LEAVING THE
MARKETPLACE
FOR MINISTRY

CAREER CROSSOVER

B&H
PUBLISHING GROUP
Nashville, Tennessee

TOM R. HARPER

ISBN: 978-0-8054-4441-4

Published by B & H Publishing Group,
Nashville, Tennessee

Dewey Decimal Classification: 253.2
Subject Heading: PASTORAL THEOLOGY
                   CAREER CHANGES
                   VOCATIONAL GUIDANCE

1 2 3 4 5 6 7 8 9 10   11 10 09 08 07

To Dad—who believed in me to the end

IIIIIIIIIIIII

Contents

||||||||||||||

Foreword

I wish I had had this book in my hand twenty-two years ago. As you will read shortly, I was a banker who loved my job. For months I could not understand why God was giving me an uneasy spirit about my vocation. Why was I no longer sensing that fulfillment that came with my work? Why did I have these crazy ideas about going to seminary and entering a path of vocational ministry?

Ultimately, I did leave the bank and enter seminary. After four pastorates, a dozen years as a dean of a large seminary, and serving as the CEO of the largest Christian resource company in the world, I can say without hesitation that I have no regrets. The ride has been incredible.

But the ride has not always been easy.

It seemed as if I had a plethora of questions that no one could answer. I remember when I told my mother of my call to ministry, she asked a straightforward question: "How will you make a living for your family at seminary?" Mom and Dad obviously were enjoying the freedom-from-dependents life stage and had no intention of returning to the era of financially supporting a child. I responded with a blank stare. I did not have an answer.

I met Tom Harper several years ago. He bounded into my office with unbridled enthusiasm. He had so many questions about so many issues. We ultimately entered into a business partnership that continued until I came to LifeWay Christian Resources in 2005.

On many occasions Tom would ask me questions about my crossover from the business world to the vocational ministry. His questions were obviously more than a passing interest. He was really curious and fascinated about stories of people who had transitioned from the so-called secular world to the world of vocational ministry. And when Tom found out that I had traveled that path, he peppered me with a series of great and insightful questions.

At the time Tom saw me as an exception, perhaps even an oddity. Like many, his perception was that vocational ministers go directly from high school to Bible college and perhaps seminary. They rarely go another path.

But I was not the only person of whom he began to ask questions. And the more ministers he spoke to, the more he realized that career crossovers were not as unusual as he originally suspected.

Tom's interest evolved into a major research project and the book you now have in your hands. And as I read this book, I soon realized that it should be read by two major audiences. First, the logical readership includes those who are considering a career crossover or who may be in the process of such a move. I would have been well served to have these facts and stories in front of me twenty-five years ago.

But a second major audience should be those who are interested in the paths and struggles of their pastors and ministers. That may include laypersons in the church or other ministers.

I can only see a church getting stronger by understanding the background and the heart of career crossover ministers.

Be forewarned before you begin reading *Career Crossover:* the book is difficult to put down. I blame Tom Harper for at least two nights of poor sleep. This may be a research project, but it is anything but boring. The facts are intriguing and the stories are fascinating.

Thanks, Tom, for doing a great service for so many people who have traveled or will travel the path I once traveled. But, above all, thanks for making such a great contribution to the Church and to the Kingdom.

Thom S. Rainer
President and CEO
LifeWay Christian Resources

|||||||||||||

Acknowledgments

When I was in high school, my desire to be published was as strong as any emotion or ambition in life. I used to write snippets during class and had a few devoted "fans" that read along the way. I appreciate your holding back most of the criticism, guys. And thanks for encouraging me with your interest!

The most significant and long-term encouragement came from my parents, particularly Dad. Supportive to the core, he became my first editor (starting around fifth grade) and actually granted me a bona fide loan to pay for a book doctor several years later. I still have the official promissory note somewhere. Because I had never signed a financial contract before, the stress mounted as I tentatively scratched my name on the line. He told me there were severe penalties for people like me who defaulted on loans.

Several unpublished novels later, Dad's support never wavered. Sadly, he was diagnosed with liver cancer in February of 2004 and passed away less than a month later. Of course this stunned our entire family and his many friends throughout the safety industry, which he had served for several decades. Since then my mother has been blessed with a blossoming faith—isn't it amazing what God can do with tragedies?

Mom, thanks for embarrassing me with your cheers from the sidelines. And Stace, thanks for being a godly sister whose spiritual maturity still leaves me in amazement.

Dr. Thom Rainer, your encouragement, friendship, and the introduction to your new colleagues at B & H opened a door for which I'll always be grateful. Jim Weaver, acquisitions editor at Kregel Publications—your gracious guidance got me off the ground with this project. I look forward to meeting up some day. Rebecca Barnes, thanks for your assistance with chapter 4, and Bob Browning—your encouragement and tireless work are one of my secret assets. Cindy and Matt at Starbucks, thanks for fueling my creativity with a smile and a "venti" whenever I plugged into my second office!

And most importantly, I extend soul-felt gratitude to my wife Karen, who put up with my youthful dreams and loved me through them. I praise the Lord for using you to bring me to Christ and for helping me grow up in him.

INTRODUCTION

Confessions
of a Pastor Wannabe

Our Western culture unfairly divides ministry and the workplace into separate callings. Many believe that if you're in a secular work environment, you surely can't be in any kind of direct ministry—and that a businessperson who changes his stripes can't be an effective full-time pastor or missionary.

Our team conducted an extensive research project to study this intriguing group of improbable crossover pastors. Out of the 738 respondents in our first survey, we discovered a startling trend: nearly half (44 percent) of senior pastors and ministers once worked in the secular marketplace. If you're one of them, or you're thinking about joining their numbers, this book is for you.

You may have heard about the "kingdom entrepreneurs" that set up businesses in Third World countries. Their sharp business skills and prayerful ministry goals coexist with impressive results. They're welcomed by the host countries because they provide jobs, training, exports, and other blessings to needy populations. Governments tend to overlook the entrepreneurs' missionary activities in light of their legitimate economic output. I hope and pray this "business as mission" trend continues.

A reality we face in the West, however, is that our dualistic mind-sets have a hard time coupling the two concepts; we espouse "business *or* mission." We don't believe business ventures can be spiritual because of the common unbiblical misconception that money is a necessary evil. This error is reinforced when we take time from our jobs (i.e., the world of money) to serve people engulfed in poverty. Several friends of mine who came home from Third World countries were embarrassed by our culture's materialism.

I was shocked to learn so many church leaders hailed from the workplace. Business missionaries in other parts of the world were one thing, but businessmen turned ministers in the U.S. surely ran counter to reality. Most of the marketplace leaders I know strive for success, so they can fatten their tithe or support parachurch ministries.

These crossover people pursue their dream, but I still toy with mine. I'm still in business, harboring a longtime secret desire to enter the ministry, though I admit the dream has faded as God has continued to reveal his plans for me. But in spite of my lack of giftedness and training in preaching—along with my huge to-do list and harried days—I still wonder how hard I'd grip the wooden edges of a pulpit, whether anyone would respond to my gospel presentation, and how many I would baptize through the years.

Is that how you feel?

Where are you in *your* dream? Do you own a body shop, sell clothes, run a help desk, tend a bank counter, groom dogs, manage a human resources department, build Web sites, sell pharmaceuticals, write commercials, or run a multinational corporation?

Do you get up every day and go to a job that sometimes seems insignificant or meaningless? Have you dreamed of leading a church that reaches the lost? If you volunteer at your church, does your heart gravitate toward *leading* rather than just *participating?*

You've got plenty of company. Hundreds of thousands have made the jump from the workplace to full-time ministry before you. Some stuck their toes in the water before committing. Others dove head first and trusted God for their survival. Still others made the leap perhaps too soon.

Many marketplace-to-ministry crossovers responded to our survey with inspiring stories of transformation and adventure. This book is full of amazing and encouraging accounts of people who embraced their calls.

If you've got similar designs on crossing over, be careful. Before you jump the fence, there are certain questions you should ask yourself and scriptural requirements you should pass. There are keys to financial planning that could provide for your family while your ministry gathers steam. You'll need to unlearn some marketplace habits and adjust your mind-set to a whole new world.

In this book you'll read advice, encouragement, and wisdom from the candid personal accounts of dozens of pastors. Our research yielded a wealth of tips that will save time and help you cast a realistic vision for your own switch to ministry.

Most of all, amid all the warnings and advice, you must not lose that simmering desire to add significance to your life. However God directs you from here, he has a plan for your life's work. Whether you've already crossed over into ministry, just started thinking about it, or are in the middle of a marketplace-to-ministry shift, I pray this book will encourage your steps.

God uses our Western dualism for his own purposes. He calls myriad people from the marketplace. And if God has called you to lead or work in a church or ministry, he will surely equip you. He has prepared work for you that fits perfectly with your skills, passions, and experiences.

If you hear a call in your life, investigate it. Pray. Discuss. Plan.

If you'd like expert advice from those who have already realized their dreams, read on.

1
||||||||||||||

Business or Ministry: What Should You *Do* with Your Life?

*God has many of his people in business to reach
the lost around them . . . But if he wants you to make a
radical change in your career, well, he'll make that clear.*

—SURVEY RESPONDENT

I f you peruse any bookstore, Christian or not, you could walk
away discouraged and amazed.

Discouraged because the plethora of books about what
to do with your life stare back at you with accusing, demean-
ing gazes. *Don't you know what in the world you're here for?*
they seem to demand. *Buy me and let's talk.*

I have nothing against the many excellent, biblical books
about discovering God's plan for our lives. What amazes me is
that their staggering number grows every year.

Not that it was the first on the topic, but Rick Warren's
The Purpose-Driven Life seems to have spawned a new literary
niche. His powerful book sold tens of millions of copies and
broke publishing records. But the public was not satisfied with

his "forty purposes." They still hungered. Publishers, sensing a groundswell of meaningless lives, continued to churn out title after purpose-filled title.

And we bought them.

Bob Buford's *Halftime*, published in the midnineties, helped me understand that my yearning for significance was a widespread phenomenon. If you feel a midlife dissatisfaction with work, as I did, your mind will race with new possibilities and purposes after you read it. I learned practical ways to strategize leaving my mark and glorifying Christ before I check out.

After I read that book, I realized I knew many pastors and church consultants who had left the business world. Many told me they felt "called" to drop their secular worklife and pick up an uncertain future. Their faith humbled me. Their boldness encouraged me.

But I wanted to learn more. As I mentioned in the introduction, my team conducted a survey of people who currently serve in vocational ministry. We found that more than a third of all church leaders and workers had transitioned out of the marketplace. Not only had thousands of secular employees unwrapped the gift of God's purpose for their lives, they had decided to uproot their families, revolutionize their lives, and step into a daunting unknown.

And gave up great sums of money to do so.

WHY THIS BOOK IS "NEXT"

Career Crossover will not lead you on a journey of discovery for the meaning of your existence. But it will lead you on a journey into the ministry, if you're so inclined.

If you're not just glancing over these first few pages but have actually bought this book, you're seriously considering the ministry. Let me also presume you want some practical information and advice on how and when to make this move. And it would be nice to know what to expect along the way, wouldn't it?

Hundreds of thousands currently in ministry hailed from the marketplace. I've heard admonitions from authors and pastors that you should stay where you are and minister to your workmates. That's great advice. But the numbers tell me that next year thousands will feel so strongly about full-time ministry that they'll jump in within months of their decision.

If you might be one of those jumpers, pause for a few breaths and learn from those who have jumped before you. If you're not content with your job and wonder if God might be calling you to become a pastor, worship leader, or church administrator, heed the nuggets of wisdom from other cross-over leaders.

This book's pages are filled by our 344 research respondents who shared volumes of inspiring advice, personal struggles, and amazing journeys. They volunteered intimate insights about themselves—spiced at times with humor—that could have filled many more books.

One of the respondents, Pastor Jeff Daxon, said something that excites me every time I read it: "While many men my age are wondering if they have done the right things with their life, I am finding my greatest fulfillment. God gave me a passion for teaching and ministry. He then gave me the courage to chase that passion."

Wouldn't you give your left arm to say that and mean it? Jeff is living out his calling. He enjoys life because he loves his work and he's exercising his God-given gifts. How many of us, even after a life of following what we believe is the Lord's plan, can report as much satisfaction?

Sadly, many study respondents can point to numerous past mistakes. They can list several regrets, missteps, and sins.

Jeff's own road to bliss took several detours. In fact, our team didn't find any leaders who coasted into their ministry without wrong turns or outright accidents. So take note: you *will* slam into—or at least trip over—obstacles.

ABOUT THE MARKETPLACE-TO-MINISTRY RESEARCH PROJECT

Our survey did not meet enough criteria to earn a "scientific" label by the experts, but our 344 respondents decreased the margin of error to within plus or minus 5 percent. This survey and an earlier study (with 738 responses, as mentioned in the introduction) produced many of the key statistics in this book.

We were overwhelmed by the detailed, heartfelt responses to our open-ended questions. To these generous leaders we owe deep gratitude. Their insights, combined with the voluminous data, tell compelling stories. Hearing some of them in person ignited my own passion for the work of the ministry.

You'll probably get tired of hearing my favorite statistic: *38 percent of all church leaders came from the secular marketplace.* This number represents roughly 380,000 people in the U.S. alone. We estimate millions worldwide left business for ministry. While this is certainly not a new trend, I haven't seen any other books on the topic.

We combed through reams of interesting data to find common strains of successful crossover leaders. But the real color showed up in the subjective questions. You're going to read fascinating comments and anecdotes in response to the following questions:

- What were the biggest obstacles you faced in making this transition?
- What do you regret most, if anything, about your decision to cross over?
- What has been your biggest frustration in ministry that you did not face in the business world?
- What workplace skills have proven most helpful to you in ministry?
- *What is the most important advice you can give to people considering leaving their job or career for ministry work?*

The last question encompasses the theme of this book. You should leave these pages with a clearer picture of your own transition plan—or, if it is not God's will, you may decide that a move into ministry lacks the attraction it once held.

While the actual job titles of the respondents varied, the top four categories break down like this:

- full-time pastor/minister, 47 percent
- church staff member, 14 percent
- part-time pastor/minister, 11 percent
- parachurch/nonprofit, 10 percent

I had the pleasure of organizing the wisdom of these people into chapters, but I will let many of their own words shine through. I've highlighted many of their quotes for quick reference when you need a shot of encouragement down the pike.

A WORD ABOUT THE PARACHURCH

Throughout this book you will find me referring to pastors and other church leaders, but I don't want to ignore an important segment of God's workforce: the parachurch.

This interesting animal is defined and studied in the book *The Prospering Parachurch: Enlarging the Boundaries of God's Kingdom* by Willmer, Schmidt, and Smith (Jossey-Bass, 1998). The authors call the parachurch a "paradigm shift for the church." By definition, a parachurch is a specialized institutional ministry standing outside the structure of established religious bodies. And because it's free from the strings of hierarchy and church bureaucracy, it operates with a great degree of flexibility with regard to innovation and change. The Billy Graham Evangelistic Association is the best example of a well-known parachurch. Other types include Bible tract societies, seminaries and colleges, missionary groups, campus ministries, religious broadcasters, social services, rescue missions, camps, prison ministries, and moral reform organizations.

Since there are many more churches than parachurches, I won't talk too much about this type of organization. But certainly the same principles will apply to either sector as you ponder the ministry, and for many marketplace people, the parachurch promises a more businesslike environment compared to the average small church.

The following research tidbits and the comments throughout this book include people who work in parachurches, but the majority serve directly in a congregational setting either on staff or as a volunteer.

FIVE SURPRISES ABOUT CROSSOVER LEADERS

We encountered many surprising facts and comments in the survey results. The following five points will give you a brief glimpse into some of the lifestyles, habits, and mind-sets of the respondents.

1. *Before they crossed over, the leaders were not concentrated in a few top industries.* I expected to see clusters come from markets like retail, legal, or sales, but the results showed a much broader spread. Some of the least popular preministry careers were the military, purchasing/procurement, restaurant/food service, science, and sports.

"Whatever you are leaving is going to pale in comparison to what God has in store for you in ministry. He will use you and your gifts for his kingdom work." — Survey respondent

---

2. *Twenty-seven percent still work part- or full-time in a secular job.* This reflects a common comment about the financial difficulty many faced when they pursued their calling. More than a quarter of the respondents found a happy medium between leaving their job outright and diving into low-paying (or no-paying) ministry. No one said you had to go cold turkey.

3. *Forty-one percent had been Christian for more than twenty-five years before crossing over and had been in their previous industry for more than sixteen years.* This is a mature group, both professionally and spiritually. We thought this important career decision was more common to new Christians still fired up about their

newfound faith. Instead we found a refreshing cadre of mentors willing to share their experiences with others. Pastor Daxon said, "With my professional experience in management, international travel, consulting and problem solving, I felt that there must be a kingdom use for what God had orchestrated in my life."

4. *Many were greatly influenced by their pastor.* When asked, "Who did God use to most influence your decision?" the top two responses, at 29 percent each, were "senior pastor/minister" and "no one in particular." The third top answer was "spouse" at 14 percent.

5. *The deliberation before finalizing a decision to leave the marketplace was extremely short.* We thought the decision-making process was more drawn out. Instead we learned that this is a determined, decisive bunch. Sixty-nine percent thought about their decision for a year or less before settling on their direction. But here are the real shockers within that group:

   Length of deliberation before decision:

   2–4 weeks .... 11 percent

   1–7 days .... 8 percent

   A matter of hours .... 9 percent

Some people felt the calling, thought about their options, prayed for wisdom, and committed to a life shift *in the time it'll take you to finish this book.* I don't recommend such quick movement, but it does happen.

"After making my decision, I was more at peace with myself than ever before in my life." —Survey respondent

---

Before you start planning your career switch and signing up for seminary classes, take another breath, nestle into your seat, and direct an attentive ear to one of the most important areas our research uncovered. It may just change your mind.

POINTS TO PONDER

1. Have you read a "life purpose" book like Rick Warren's *The Purpose-Driven Life?* See appendix 3 for a list of similar titles.

2. If you're serious about investigating the ministry as your full-time work, have you decided whether you'd like to work on staff at a church, in a parachurch, as a nonprofit volunteer, in consulting, or in some other specific ministry? See appendixes 1 and 2 for actual job descriptions of key church positions and an overview of the church consulting field.

2
||||||||||||

God May Not Want You to Cross Over ... Yet

The one who works his land will have plenty of food,
but whoever chases fantasies lacks sense.
–PROVERBS 12:11

There is a corporate ladder in the ministry world.

Many crossover leaders try to climb it, seeking the same fame and monetary gain they chased in the marketplace. If they become senior pastor of a growing church, the headiness of speaking to hundreds or thousands of devotees from the pulpit every week and seeing a swelling budget can make humility difficult. They're finally CEO of their church. This may be their closest brush with being the big cheese.

Why do *you* want to enter the ministry?

Why in the world would you leave your current life and career to serve ungrateful sheep, face financial difficulty, suffer biting criticism, and endure long hours and short vacations?

Of course, I could've asked the same question of a minister thinking about secular work. And that's my point—the two worlds are more alike than you think. It seems that on either side of the fence, the greener grass loses its luster the longer you stand on it. Picture yourself several years into your ministry, on one of your worst days when a deacon openly undermines your leadership, and see if you still love your job. I'm sure you've had plenty of similar days no matter where you work.

Good reasons abound for entering the ministry. But you'll want to figure out *your* reasons first—don't assume you heard a call today then blindly jump tomorrow. Our respondents suggested ten *bad* reasons to leave life in the marketplace:

1. You're discouraged and burned-out in your current job.
2. You want to feel good about your work.
3. You feel the need to please someone else (family, friends, etc.).
4. You dream of "changing the world."
5. You failed at other jobs and want to try something new.
6. You want a "career" in the church.
7. You're low on funds and think church work would be easy money for awhile.
8. You think ministry seems like the most fun job out of several you're considering.
9. You want to try your hand at full-time ministry to see if you like it.
10. You see an open church position that has better hours, benefits, or salary than your current position.

Do these questions induce a nod or two? If so, your calling may originate more from yourself than the Lord.

WHAT SEASON ARE YOU IN?

If you feel led to leave the hotbed of spiritual outreach—the marketplace—our survey respondents want to catch you for a word or two before you leave.

Jesus himself worked in the family carpentry business. Many of his teachings were parables that resonated with business people and the entire working class. Two thousand years ago, the average adult life revolved around work and business transactions—no different from today.

Our Lord worked longer in business than he did in full-time ministry. This was no accident—he easily identified with those in the marketplace and with secular workers through the ages. He not only crossed over, he spun business into deeply significant lessons and illustrations.

God placed you in your current career because it is a season of your life that has a beginning and an end ordained by him. A preacher friend of mine, Dan Hall, delivered a sermon recently on God's perfect timing. He pondered why Jesus appeared on the earth in that exact moment in history. Why didn't he come earlier, before the Egyptian enslavement? Or later, right before the fall of Jerusalem?

We can't guess at God's reasons for his timing. But he has ordained a place in time for everything, especially his Son's birth: "While they were there, *the time came* for her [Mary] to give birth. Then she gave birth to her firstborn Son" (Luke 2:6–7, my emphasis).

In Ecclesiastes 3:1, Solomon writes, "There is an occasion for everything, / and a time for every activity under heaven."

Is a season about to end—or begin—in your life? Or is the time not yet ripe for any changes?

If we would only trust that the Lord brought us into our current season for a limited time to learn specific lessons, to grow in our walk, to serve certain people—then we would enjoy the moment. We can have faith that our Father in heaven will carry us into the next chapter of our lives at just the right time.

One crossover leader made this point: "Be faithful with what God *has* put in front of you before you consider being faithful with what you *want* God to put in front of you. If you aren't salt and light now, don't assume you will be salt and light in vocational ministry either."

Bloom where you're planted, says the adage. Extend your roots deep into the dirt under your feet. Practice ministering in a familiar environment. Witness to people you know.

"Be certain that God isn't just calling you to become more active in ministry right where you are. The business world is a wonderful place to do ministry, and you don't have to have an 'MDiv' after your name to reach out to the world around you." — Survey respondent

LIFESTORY

Doug Spada—
From Submariner to Entrepreneur to Worklife Minister
Age at crossover: 33
Former position: Entrepreneur/ military
Company: Utili-Tech Inc.
Key quote: "Most believers influence a majority of the unchurched world not through church activity

and ministry, but through their ministry and witness in the workplace!"

"It was 1994. I was checking into a hotel in La Mesa, California, alone, separated from my wife. Our marriage was ripped apart—littered with pain, abuse, and selfishness. While in one sense I had it all—business success and money—in the most important ways I had nothing, and my struggle centered around one huge question, What is my calling in life?

"I was raised going to church, but I never really understood 'the God thing.' I tried to do all the right things and look all the right ways, but I had a void in my life. I did not understand God's desire for me to receive his forgiveness or his calling and direction for my worklife. I had grown up hearing people say things like, 'I have been called to preach,' or, 'I have been called to be a missionary.' I never heard anyone say they were called to a job. So I wondered where that left me—and the rest of us—in the workplace.

"Vocationally, I have a military background in nuclear engineering. I helped operate fast attack submarines for almost a decade. Then I started an energy cost-management company in San Diego and enjoyed great success. But I had this nagging issue. I wanted to be significant, and I wanted to feel called by God to my work. God then began to move in my life in some dramatic ways, and I sensed he was calling me—but to what?

"Dr. Henry Blackaby wrote, 'There is nothing worse than a great calling with a weak character.' Calling and character have to work as a team, and that scared me because I knew I had huge character deficits. I realized God was not just looking at what I could *do* for him but at my character. Despite my huge character flaws, God kept pursuing me, asking me to surrender to him.

"This just intensified the turmoil in my life, however. I finally surrendered my life to whatever God wanted. Little did I know, great sacrifice was right before me.

"When I checked into the hotel that night, life seemed over for me. But when I walked into the room, I flipped on the light and on the nightstand was a Bible, already opened, calling for me to read it. With my heart beating wildly, I walked over and looked down at the open pages. As I read, God breathed life and purpose into me, and I became his.

"The Bible was opened to Isaiah 43:1–3. I felt the Lord speaking directly to me:

'Do not fear, for I have redeemed you;
I have called you by your name; you are Mine.
I will be with you
when you pass through the waters,
and [when you pass] through the rivers,
they will not overwhelm you.
You will not be scorched
when you walk through the fire,
and the flame will not burn you.
For I the LORD your God,
the Holy One of Israel, and your Savior,
give Egypt as a ransom for you,
Cush and Seba in your place.'

"That night changed my life. I was called by God to be his! But I still had this other 'calling' question. What was I to do with my life and work?

"My logical assumption was to be as spiritually significant as possible. For me, that meant I had to quit my job. I tried hard to join the church staff to 'fulfill the ultimate calling,' but God kept blocking me. I did not understand why I couldn't serve in this way. I [fell] into a private depression, [confused] about the issues of faith, work, and calling. I wondered if my work had anything to do with my calling from God or was divine calling just for a chosen few?

"Through much more brokenness, God began to guide me to truths that have freed me. I realized that my spiritual gifting has everything to do with my vocational work and not just work in the church. I realized that my work was a holy calling no matter what it was—if I worked for God.

"I realized that work was not cursed. God is a worker, and he invites me to join him in his creative work in this world. I realized there is no biblical separation of work as either 'sacred' or 'secular.'

"Finally, I understood that I was free to serve God through my work. I was called! He led me to start a ministry called HisChurchatWork.org to help local churches equip and release their people to fulfill *their* ministry in and through the work-place. We provide the local church with a sustainable model for worklife ministry, including biblical teaching and resources that encourage and mobilize believers into their God-given calling of work.

"I didn't have to leave the workplace and join a church or ministry to fulfill my calling. Sometimes God will keep your feet planted in the workplace—or in my case, between the church and the workplace, joining their hands together. This is right where I need to be, where I feel the Lord's will for my life."

THE "MARKETPLACE MINISTRY" TREND

In recent years, a groundswell of workplace ministry initiatives has transformed thousands of Christian businesspeople into on-the-job missionaries. My own church, Southeast Christian in Louisville, Kentucky, reaches out to the business community through its Worklife Ministry that Doug Spada helped create for the church. The program teaches the arts of interviewing, job hunting, and witnessing to colleagues.

I used to think you had to be either in business *or* ministry and that the twain would never meet—the whole separation-of-church-and-state thing. I gave part of my earnings to the church, so they could do their work while I did mine. I promised to give the church as much time as I could spare. But years passed and my time didn't provide for much volunteer work.

I've since learned that the marketplace can integrate *with* the work of the church. The book *On Kingdom Business* by Tetsunao Yamamori and Kenneth A. Eldred (Crossway, 2003) observes that evangelistic entrepreneurs, or "kingdom professionals," have mastered the art of setting up for-profit companies that simultaneously minister as part of everyday operations.

These resourceful, zealous businesspeople find a geographic area in need of economic revitalization, usually in a Third World country. They then bless that impoverished region with jobs, vocational skills training, export product sales, community leadership, access to new imports, tithes for local church support, and an overall economic boost.

The other half of their mission is to plant churches, evangelize, shepherd new believers, teach the Bible, and advance the kingdom of God. Many of these pioneers are welcomed even by Muslim governments because of their legitimate business benefits.

What a great strategy: engage in the Lord's earthly work by touching the lives of people, supporting the church, and witnessing for Christ.

You can do that right now . . . in your current job . . . with your surrounding coworkers . . . without packing up for a long trip into the poverty-stricken unknown . . . yet.

A STORY OF WORKPLACE WITNESSING

When I sold advertising for a rock radio station in the midnineties, I formed a quick friendship with a new ad rep a few cubicles down from mine. He overflowed with positive energy and laid several hints that he might be a Christian. I was a relatively new believer myself, so this excited me.

We started doing lunch. I found out he was a Jehovah's Witness. I panicked.

I soon became a target for his smooth words and sound arguments against what I knew to be true. But I also started reading about how to counter his tactics. We had some healthy debates. I hungered for further equipping. Finally I enrolled in a seminary class on witnessing to the cults.

As a grad student I was assigned an end-of-term paper on any topic within the scope of the class. I spent an evening of indecision about my theme. The next day, God sent two young Witnesses literally to my doorstep, and my paper turned into an account of the ensuing conversations with my new Jehovah's Witness friends.

My growing passion for apologetics and the cults started with a workplace relationship. God used my friend to give me depth and awaken a hunger for learning. In the end that coworker indirectly equipped me to break more effectively through the deceptions of cults.

If you leave your secular career, what opportunities will you squander that God meant only for you? Are there people around you at work right now who need to hear the gospel?

"Don't buy into the flawed head space that business is 'secular' and ministry is 'sacred.' There's no such dichotomy. I've learned that those in the marketplace have many more opportunities to impact the lost for Jesus than I do as a pastor."　　　　　　　　　— Survey respondent

---

Does God want you to walk away from the ministry he's developing for you on the job? Maybe he wants you to ask him right now, before you go any further with your dream.

THE SPIRITUAL VALUE OF THE MARKETPLACE

American culture separates church and work into oil and water.

But work of any kind can glorify God, serve the community, support the families of employees, provide income for suppliers, offer hard-to-find products in an isolated town, meet the practical needs of customers, produce materials that others can use for profit, and feed taxes to the government that supports the military, police, fire and emergency protection, roads and highways, public transportation—and the benefit chain goes on.

Business also provides a source of funding for churches and charities that serve the community. The gospel spreads through work relationships. The marketplace feeds an economic food chain that makes society tick. Companies improve the quality of life by providing jobs and meaningful work.

The working world sets off a string of dominoes within God's will that links events and people in a series of chain reactions. Without this network, many basic human needs would remain unmet, and Christians would not have as many opportunities to reach the lost.

Ken Blanchard sold millions of copies of his best seller *The One Minute Manager.* Years later he sold out to Jesus and was inspired with an idea to speak to thousands about the most successful biblical leadership principles ever modeled. Talk about a marketplace-to-ministry transformation.

The crowds of Christian leaders that attend Ken's "Lead Like Jesus" conferences dig down into the grass roots of their local communities with the message of Christ. They exemplify servanthood. Many nonbelievers see Jesus in these marketplace leaders . . . and watch very closely.

"My wife is in the health care sector. I often wish I had the ministry opportunities to touch the lives of undecided people that she has."

—Survey respondent

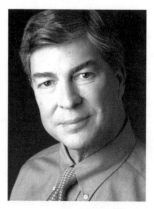

LIFESTORY

Bob Buford—
From Media Mogul
to Social Entrepreneur
Age at crossover: 45
Former position: CEO
Company: Buford Television
Key quote: "It's utterly a matter of calling."

Bob Buford brought the concept of *halftime* into sharp focus for a multitude of men and women facing midlife searches for purpose. His book *Halftime* delves into the mind of the middle-aged achiever who wants to make a mark—not just money—in this world.

Bob's recent work, *Finishing Well*, puts retirement into perspective. He interviewed 120 accomplished people, most of whom scoffed at the mention of retirement. Though in the world's eyes they deserved to slow down and relax a little, they couldn't stop serving others with their God-given talents and passions as long as they were able.

Bob's own journey is a little different from most you'll read in this book. I found his second-half work intriguing—author, speaker, head of Leadership Network (which connects innovators within the world of large churches), life coach, and participant in numerous boards and other distinguished groups. Like him, I feel God has given me certain skills and a personality that don't fit the pastor or church-staff mold. I feel drawn toward organizational and creative work rather than preaching or teaching. I would love to go on a mission trip or help a bold pastor plant a church, but full-time leadership in a local church doesn't seem to be the Lord's vision for me.

When I interviewed him, I was struck by Bob's obvious heart for people trying to discern the next chapter in their lives. I posed an objection to him that I'd heard from other respected and well-known leaders: "What do you think about those who say we shouldn't necessarily look for significance outside of our job, but instead seek ways to minister to those around us in our current careers? In other words, do you agree that God gives us certain spheres of influence he wants us to reach without leaving the marketplace?"

"It's utterly a matter of calling," he said.

I'll let him explain.

SHOULD YOU STAY . . . OR GO?

During his last eight years as CEO of Buford Television, Bob worked on transitioning into his own halftime until he sold the family-owned national cable company in 1999. When he wrote *Halftime*, he was still four years away from leaving the marketplace to become a social entrepreneur.

"When I came to halftime," he says, "I wanted to re-allocate 80 percent of myself to kingdom things. A lot of the people I see who make a crossover do it the way I did—through a parallel career. What you do is begin what I call 'low-cost probes,' where you try some things out and you see whether they work for you."

While we should take our time finding the right fit, we shouldn't "endlessly stew" about our direction, he says. Some people fantasize that some day their ticket will arrive, and they can finally realize their dreams of serving others and following God's will for their lives. But too often the daydream passes because they can't pry themselves away from life's busyness—jobs, young kids, bills, and an addiction to the pursuit of success.

"In my case, I had a very measured course," Bob says. "It took maybe eight years to get most of me transferred into a ministry."

After he started Leadership Network, he remained chairman of his company's board. He crafted an abbreviated role for himself, focusing mostly on the company's mission and values. He came into the office once or twice a month.

THE OBSTACLES TO SIGNIFICANCE

In *Finishing Well*, Bob's interviewees faced three common obstacles while seeking their higher purpose. The first was creating enough balance in life before trying something more significant—without abandoning their current commitments. The second was realizing their role in the business world was often different from their core gifts and talents. The third challenge was figuring out exactly *how* to "do" significance.

In Bob's case, he created a role as a social entrepreneur and created Leadership Network. His second "significance" activity—about ten years later—was writing *Halftime*, which helped fund his new direction.

"Perhaps the overarching and more general constraint is self-sufficiency, the sense that you can do this all yourself," he says. "I think the first line in Rick Warren's book *The Purpose-Driven Life* is a watershed kind of statement. He says, 'It's not about you.' And if you really think too much that it is about you, it's like you're trying to run a car without the engine. Particularly in the area of doing God's work, it's about God's purposes and our willingness to submit to them."

A MATTER OF CALLING

Now back to the question: if God directs our paths (Prov. 3:6), why should we take it upon ourselves to leave our jobs and go into ministry?

Bob believes Jesus ministered to people in his own path: the woman at the well, Zacchaeus in the tree, Martha and Mary. "I think you can fully do that [minister where you are] in business. You can do pastoral care all day long with just the customers and coworkers and other people."

But, he says, you can't plant churches while you're also a CEO. You can't be committed to both your job and what you believe is your calling unless one of them takes a backseat while you focus on the other.

"Peter Drucker once asked me how much I was involved in my business and how much I was involved in ministry. I said it was probably fifty-fifty. And he said, 'That's just wrong. You either need to be involved 80 percent in your business or 20 percent in your business.' By that he meant if you're in charge, you need to be guiding things in a very active way—involved, not distant. But the worst [thing] is to just *say* you've delegated that responsibility and in fact you cling to it. You don't give enough of yourself to really do it well and you don't give [less] of yourself to let someone else do it well."

Bob predicts an increasing number of leaders will move from the marketplace to full-time ministry. "The two trends that I see mostly are planting new churches, which usually involves marketplace people, and the other one is starting multi-venue churches, where a home church has satellite locations. Life Covenant Church in Edmond, Oklahoma, had five hundred people attending eight years ago in one location. About three years ago, they had seven thousand people attending at five locations, and they now have eleven thousand people at even more sites. At the time they had the seven thousand people attending, they had seventy-two full-time staff, of whom seventy-one had a marketplace background."

Whether we minister in the marketplace or enter ministry, Bob emphatically believes God's personal call on our lives determines our individual paths. But, he says, "either one of those callings is equally valid."

The Call Still Comes

Bob Buford's story supports a fact shown by our research: though a huge number of Christians minister where they work, thousands will leap into full-time ministry each year. The call to cross over obviously compels many to uproot and commit to a new life.

God's plan for each person is so unique and specific that only *you* can discern what's right for you. Listen to God, pray, read the Word, seek wise counsel, talk to your pastor, and include your family in your decision. Don't rely on your gut or your emotions to decide. Intuition should only get your thinking started.

Many ministry leaders said that all their skills, experiences, failures, successes, relationships, and lessons equipped them perfectly for their specific ministry mission.

One respondent's skill set transferred largely intact: "As a lawyer, my job was to read, study, gather evidence, persuade, challenge, and defend. I do that all the time as a pastor. As a lawyer, I spent my life mediating and seeking to resolve conflict. I have used those skills hugely in the church—almost daily."

Let's examine an important, practical first step toward understanding if you and the ministry really fit.

What Is Your Dream?

The crossover ministers in our study advised that you make this transition only if you can't imagine serving God in any other way except full-time ministry.

The number of comments on this issue was over-whelming:

"If you can be happy in your current position, or in another profession, do not consider the ministry."

"If there is a way to pursue your calling and exercise your spiritual gifts without entering into full-time ministerial service, do it."

"If you can do anything else in life besides working in the ministry and you are satisfied with it, do it."

"If you can have peace and not be in ministry, then don't be."

"Don't do it unless you have exhausted every opportunity to minister in the marketplace or until the call from the Lord is so clear that you would be disobedient if you said no."

"Pursue any other profession you can until God makes it clear that your days of running are over."

—Survey respondents

Do you have peace in your current job? If you stayed in the working world but changed jobs, would you finally find happiness?

Top life coaches like Laurie Beth Jones pose a question that carries incredible significance: If money were no object, and you could do anything you wanted with your life, what would that be?

What is your dream?

Is your answer "ministry"?

If so, your next step is to put your dream to the test. The great thing is you don't have to leave your job to find out if you're cut out for the ministry. If you're not sure whether your dream is God's will, the following strategy is a safe next step on your road of discovery.

"I would first 'apprentice' in the area of ministry."

"First volunteer to get a feel for ministry work. You must realize that working in ministry you confront many of the same problems you may have disliked in business."

"Be actively involved in a local church in a ministry position if possible to learn the inner workings of a church."

"Is there any way you can continue your business career, even on a part-time basis, and at the same time engage in ministry?"

—Survey respondents

HOW TO TEST THE MINISTRY WATERS TO SEE IF THEY PART FOR YOU

I like how one respondent sums up this important decision: "If you can continue working in your current business career and feel at peace with God about it, then don't quit! God can certainly use you right where you are. God needs faithful business people to 'shine a light' in a world that is often dark."

If you currently have a job that pays the bills—even if your dream is very different—you are in a safe place. Be thankful God has put you in a job that provides for your basic needs. If your immediate task is to find a new job so you can more adequately cover life's expenses, my advice is to focus on securing your work before exploring your dream. You can always leave a job when you're called to move on.

Our crossovers want you to dip your toes in the water first. It is not always wise to dive into the first pool you happen upon, nor prudent to jump in without knowing how to swim.

Churches need people like you. Simply asking how you can help can set you on the path toward your future ministry with incredible speed and precision. If you already volunteer at your church, it might be time to increase your involvement to get a taste of more intense service and full-time work.

The following ideas can get you started as you sit down with your pastor, elders, or other volunteers:

- greet visitors
- serve communion
- visit the sick in hospitals
- serve in the nursery
- teach Sunday school
- work with youth
- assist your pastor with sermon research
- lead short-term mission trips
- become a deacon or elder
- volunteer as an assistant or associate pastor

Don't rush in. Try out different areas. Give time for God to grow you as you serve. Think "parallel career."

And start working on your plan.

LifeStory

Scott Vandegrift—
From Full-time Secular Job
to Half-time Church Staffer
Age at crossover: 27
Former position: Manager, Customer Support Services
Company: Gap Inc. Direct
Key quote: "Today I remain in both business and ministry."

"In the spring of 2003, after five years of management in the business world, God started speaking to me like never before. I had attended a private Baptist college in Ohio and heard the phrase 'God called me' over and over until it lost all its meaning. However, God was about to speak his own calling into my life in a surprising way.

"After joining a church plant named CrossLink Community Church in Grove City, Ohio, I became very involved in ministry. I was on the CrossLink advisory team and focused every Sunday on meeting new people, building relationships, and seeing lives change. I quickly became restless in my position at the online division of the Gap. While I had received several promotions in my short career, I felt something was missing.

"Within four months of being called, I accepted a thirty-hour-a-week position with CrossLink as their director of connection and development. It looked like this shift from business to ministry would reduce my income by half, as well as delay the starting of our family. Though my wife supported my shift into ministry, her sadness was hard to hide.

"But God had other plans. While communicating this 'career redirection' to my supervisor at the Gap, she quickly asked if I would become hourly, at the same rate, and continue working part-time for her organization. Through God's workings, I had quickly become bivocational, giving up no salary, which meant little to no sacrifice for my family. I felt like Abraham, who was willing to step out and sacrifice for God, but then was blessed simply for following God's call.

"As the next year progressed, I thought my career in the business world [would end], and I would soon go full-time into the ministry world. However, again God had other plans. Despite my part-time status at the Gap, I was soon asked to take a position that was a significant promotion, but allowed for me to stay part-time in the ministry world.

"Today I remain in both business and ministry. I continue my role at CrossLink as director of connection and leadership development, but now am also product manager of Gap Inc. Direct Contact Centers, in charge of change management and strategic direction.

"Through this bivocational setup, God has allowed me to operate in two different worlds, continue to make an impact for him in two different settings, and develop my leadership capabilities in two totally separate 'industries.'"

POINTS TO PONDER

1. Take stock of where you are in work, family, and church. Have you tried to witness and serve where you are right now? If not, why not?
2. Where could you serve in your church?
3. If money were not an issue, what kind of work would you do?

3
IIIIIIIIIIII

Nine Steps to Turning Your Decision into an Action Plan

A man's heart plans his way,
but the LORD determines his steps.
–PROVERBS 16:9

W e need ministers who are coming from the real world."
The problem with this quote from one of our respondents is that it assumes the ministry world is not "real." In fact, the ministry is just as real as the secular business world: bills still land in your mailbox, your family still needs food, cars break down, people let you down, your income isn't tied to your performance, and conflict bears its teeth with surprising ferocity.

But there's good news. You can mitigate many of these realities. I didn't say you could *escape* them, but you can soften their effect through careful preparation. The key is to plan your transition just like you'd strategize an advance against the competition, a move into a new job, a budget forecast, or a new product launch.

After we combed through reams of research for advice on taking practical steps toward full-time ministry, a blueprint for the crossover process started emerging. You may not engage the following nine steps in the exact order I've listed them. For example, you'll want to do step 4—talking to your spouse and/or family—throughout the entire process. The point is to complete all the steps. Your plan will work out like no one else's. Your skills, circumstances, and calling were gifted to you—and you alone—for a special purpose in God's greater plan.

You're about to put some meat on the bones of this calling you've been wrestling with. How would you feel with a written plan in your hands that can withstand the toughest critics and doubts and guide you on your darkest days? (Those days are coming, by the way.)

A carefully constructed plan confers three significant benefits:

1. You will quickly align your personal ministry desires and goals with God's desires for you.
2. You and your family will feel more secure knowing what life might be like over the next few years.
3. You'll feed off an inward motivation that compels you to reach your goals.

A crucial question may have entered your mind: is planning biblical? Doesn't the concept of faith—trust in God for every step in life—contradict the notion of a person mapping out his own life? (This is such a crucial question that I've devoted the next chapter to it.)

God indeed yearns for us to trust him. Consider his instructions to Moses on building the tabernacle in the book of Exodus. From crafting an acacia chest to weaving curtains out of goat hair to overlaying wood with gold, the Lord cared about every minute detail of his sanctuary on earth, issuing precise measurements for his plan: "You must make [it] according to all that I show you—the design of the tabernacle as well as the design of all its furnishings" (Exod. 25:9).

If he prepared such an exacting plan for a building, what more might he have in mind for *you*, his child? The Creator of the universe planned your life with much more detail and infinitely more love: "'For I know the plans I have for you' [this is] the LORD's declaration—'plans for [your] welfare, not for disaster, to give you a future and a hope'" (Jer. 29:11).

What a promise! Your future is in his hands, not yours. Your God knows what he's doing—not only does he see your future, he controls it. His plan is not to harm you. He has hope and prosperity in store. His plan is so much better than yours! How exciting to think he already knows where you're going, what work you're supposed to do, and how he's going to provide for all your needs.

The following steps and advice carry no guarantees. They offer only guidance and wisdom. God himself will help you discern what he might want you to know about his plan for your life. But the experiences of many leaders who have gone before you will help tune your ear to your direction from heaven.

STEP 1: PRAY AND SEARCH THE SCRIPTURES

This is the most important step by far. Don't stop seeking God's will through the two main communication channels he's opened for you. He allows us to speak directly to him and he responds to us in many ways, including and especially through his Word. He directs me to key verses at the exact time I need them. He speaks to me through other people when I least expect it. "Don't worry about anything, but in everything, through prayer and petition with thanksgiving, let your requests be made known to God" (Phil. 4:6).

He hears your every request. Part of his wisdom and guidance is found in the *process* of seeking him. Have you ever noticed that when you need a word from him on an issue in your life, you read the Bible and pray more? I do. I'm a little embarrassed by that nasty habit of mine. I should be in his Word every day. I should "pray without ceasing." I need to seek his face because of who he is, instead of knocking on his door only when I have a problem.

We are commanded by the Lord to talk with him. He doesn't *need* us, but because of his great love, he *wants* to fellowship with us. Obedience should be reason enough to pray regularly. As you cement your ministry plans, there are at least three other reasons to pray.

Reason 1—to ask for protection. The enemy may seek to thwart your entry into the ministry. He's probably already attacked you just for seriously considering it. Many who step out as bold witnesses at work suffer unexpected backlashes. Imagine the spiritual firepower leveled at you when you intensify your work for the Lord.

So pray for protection and for God's voice to drown out anyone else's. The opposition includes more than the naysayers you can see with your physical eyes. "For our battle is not against flesh and blood, but against the rulers, against the authorities, against the world powers of this darkness, against the spiritual forces of evil in the heavens" (Eph. 6:12).

Reason 2—to ask for specific direction.
This is what the Lord says:
Stand by the roadways and look.

Ask about the ancient paths:
Which is the way to what is good?
Then take it
and find rest for yourselves. (Jer. 6:16)
And whenever you turn to the right or to the left,
your ears will hear this command behind you: "This
is the way. Walk in it." (Isa. 30:21)

God made these promises to his rebellious children after they distrusted, rejected, ignored, and shamed him. They deserved his wrath. But in the midst of his threats of judgment on Israel, he told them how to escape the coming punishment and receive his favor.

We are fortunate to have Christ accept the punishment we deserve for our countless sins. And yet many times we still turn away from the Lord in our pride. We make plans without "asking where the good way is." Are you at a crossroads with your decision to enter the ministry? Are you confused about the best way to go?

When you commit your life to the Lord, when you cry to him for help, he will become that voice behind you. When you ask for the "ancient paths"—the truths found in Scripture— he will open doors and remove the obstacles under your feet.

"Think about Him in all your ways, / and He will guide you on the right paths" (Prov. 3:6). Acknowledge him through prayer. Acknowledge him by reading his Word. Seek his will and listen for his voice.

And then walk the straight path that opens up.

Reason 3—to commit your plans to the Lord. Giving your life's direction over to God requires trust and commitment. But he will reward your commitment with success. "Commit your activities to the LORD / and your plans will be achieved" (Prov. 16:3).

STEP 2: DEVELOP PERSONAL MISSION AND VISION STATEMENTS

How can we tell if a vision is from God or our own imagination? In *A Fish out of Water* by George Barna, we learn how to determine the source of our vision: "Human vision drives us to push ourselves to the limit. God's vision drives us to our knees in submission, humility and obedience." Your vision should be grand enough that only God can accomplish it. Then he will get the glory, not you.

A *vision* is defined by Ken Blanchard as *your personal, specific picture of the future that only you can live out.* God's vision for each of us is unique. But his *mission* for every Christian is the same throughout time and geography. For example, the Great Commission is for all Christ followers: "Go, therefore, and make disciples of all nations, baptizing them in the name of the Father and of the Son and of the Holy Spirit, teaching them to observe everything I have commanded you. And remember, I am with you always, to the end of the age" (Matt. 28:19–20).

If you feel drawn to the foreign mission field, your *mission* is to serve the Lord according to this passage in Matthew. Your *vision,* however, is your specific plan related to accomplishing your mission. What specific work do you want to do? Which countries will you visit? How often will you go and how long will you stay? Will you focus on your own nation instead of a foreign land? Who will work alongside you? These questions help shape your vision statement and personal assignment given by God.

SAMPLE MISSION STATEMENTS

I have read many excellent mission statements, though many tend to get confused with *vision* statements. I'm not an advocate for being didactic about *mission* versus *vision*—your plans for your future might not fit so neatly into those two boxes—but crafting a synopsis of your personal goals from two separate angles can help you measure every task in your life against your calling.

My advice is to find a mission for your life from the Bible. Make it short and back it up with memorized Scriptures. *If you plan on starting your own church or ministry, your personal mission and that of the church, given in the Bible, should be the same or similar.* If you're entering an existing ministry, closely examine its mission statement—if your personal one lines up with it, you know there's a match at the core. If you have to bend your sense of purpose around a corner to mirror the church's, the chances of your long-term job fulfillment are unfavorable.

The following sample mission statements might inspire your own:

- "To lead people into the joy of a God-centered, Bible-saturated, missions-driven life"
- "To preach the Word without compromise"
- "To evangelize the lost, edify the saved, and be a conscience to the community"
- "To exalt the Savior, equip the saints, and evangelize the sinner" (The pastor who sent us this one says, "I feel like this sums up our work as ministry leaders. My heart's desire is to truly make a difference in this world. . . . My suggestion for [those] looking for [a] mission statement is to look to where God has you and

where he is leading you. Henry Blackaby's great statement 'Go where God is' could be said in one's life as well. Where is God working in your life? Focus your mission statement in that area.")

Remember to keep your statement simple. Jesus's own mission statement is found in Luke 19:10: "For the Son of Man has come to seek and to save the lost." This is the perfect model—specific, ambitious, focused, and gospel oriented. Imagine if every pastor and every church adopted this exact mission.

SAMPLE VISION STATEMENTS

Your vision statement should flesh out your mission into specific goals. It should use your talents and passions. *It should be impossible without God's help.*

Envision yourself at the end of your life, passing your tired eyes over the years God gave you. Did you achieve God-given goals and dreams that glorified him? Did you enjoy great satisfaction and fulfillment, knowing that God's hand guided you along the way? Imagine thinking, *I ran the race God set before me—I have no regrets!*

Crafting a personal vision statement is no easy assignment and can change over time. God reserves the right to move you where he will. But a life of chasing God's vision is a life without regret.

I've listed a few visions below that may spark some ideas. Notice how each example is quantifiable, specific, and passion based:

- "To win hundreds of lost people in Louisville's West End high-crime area through an outreach-focused church and Word-based preaching"

- "To follow wherever God leads me in this world, as a Bible teacher and writer committed to connecting modern culture with the cross"
- "One by one, to reach one thousand people with the gospel before I go home to heaven"
- "To set up self-sufficient medical missionary clinics in fifty countries"
- "To save $1 million by 2020 and give it all to churches and ministries in Cuba"
- "To run successful capital campaigns for church building projects, using my network of bankers and investors"
- "To serve as a volunteer business administrator in Southland Baptist as long as I can"

Do you notice how these differ from mission statements? Only one person can accomplish these tasks. They aren't necessarily found verbatim in Scripture, but they're biblically based.

God's exciting vision for your life will ignite your passion. When you engage him, energy and joy will be balanced by peace. You'll endure hardships that he will overcome for you. You'll go to bed thinking about the next day's adventure. Pain will turn into valuable lessons and comfort for others. You'll live a full life that will be remembered by future generations.

What specific assignment has God given you? What dream will satisfy your spirit and glorify God when you look back on your life?

STEP 3: SEEK WISE COUNSEL

Do you have a circle of friends who encourage you? When I hang out with my buddies, I know they won't judge or criticize. I'm in a rare comfort zone that draws out my true self. My sarcasm flows. They accept me and I don't have to play any role except myself.

My friend Dan Hall exudes every ounce of energy he can muster. He's a fiery Baptist preacher and life coach who has worked in the church and corporate worlds and whose unique perspective on both enhances his natural ability to coach and counsel. You want to know how to confront a Christian brother in love? Ask Dan. You need guidance on dealing with poor employee morale and high turnover? Dan's your man.

But even he recognized the need for counselors and guides in his life. He created a personal board that advises him on tough decisions and issues. He hounded Bob Russell, senior minister of the twenty-thousand-member Southeast Christian Church, to mentor him. When Bob politely hinted that it might be difficult to work Dan into his hectic schedule (not mentioning the fact that they had just met), Dan put a full-court press on him until Bob agreed to start meeting over breakfast and lunch. Their friendship has grown since.

Is there a minister or successful business leader you respect? I seek the advice of others with more experience in life and ministry to broaden my perspective. And while it's easy to reap inspiration from motivational speakers, books, and even friends, balance is the key. Though you need positive energy as you plan your journey, you also need a shot of reality. Sometimes your family is the best source of both.

STEP 4: TALK TO YOUR FAMILY

The area of family communication drew the most impassioned personal comments in the research. The crossover leaders implore you to run your dreams past your family before getting too far down the planning path. With the advice came many warnings:

"Make sure you protect your time with your spouse and children. . . . You can get so busy sometimes in ministry, school, and other things that you neglect the most important thing—your relationship with God and then your family."

"I have had the misfortune of knowing three pastors whose wives were not fully behind them. Two are out of ministry completely and the other has had several bad experiences that have caused him to leave two churches in a two-year time span."

"It's important that your spouse be on board with any crazy decision like this."

"Understand that your family will live in a fishbowl."

One research stat will encourage you: when potential crossover leaders approached their families after feeling a definitive call and making a decision, the response was positive in most cases (see accompanying graph).

How did your closest family members (including spouse) respond in general to your decision?

Very positively	52.8%
Somewhat positively	29.6%
Neutral	6.1%
Somewhat negatively	8.4%
Very negatively	3.2%

The numbers probably would skyrocket into the positive if these family discussions occurred *before* the decision. Don't wait until after your decision is made to reveal it to your family.

"In all of my struggles to recognize and obey God's leading, my greatest cheerleader has been my wife. She is the sensitive one who really had to make all the sacrifices. My family was willing to change addresses and go to a new school, make new friends, etc., all because she knew God had called."
— Survey respondent

A few years ago I sensed a "calling" to go to seminary— more accurately, I had a selfish dream of winning battles with atheists and converting souls through dramatic debate. I had a banner to raise. I wanted to take blood with the sword of the Spirit. The unbelieving world was mine to conquer . . . with God's help.

After more thought and discussion with my family, I realized I hadn't thought of how it might affect them. I was lost in my own dreams and life. I craved adventure—I yearned to do battle while my family waited for me at home. In my case I was running from my obligations as a new father. The more I thought about it, the longer the list of red flags grew:

- We had a new baby—life was not going to be about me anymore.
- We planned on having more children. Therefore, life would be even *less* about me. And my extracurricular time would be even more scarce.
- My demanding job already took me away from my family—how in the world would I fit in classes, homework, studying, and writing papers?
- We had no money saved for a full master's degree program.

- I needed to grow up and realize I had real responsibilities—life wasn't about my dreams. God had given me my primary mission: my family.

"Your spouse needs to discern this call as well. In my case, my wife confirmed that God was calling us to take early retirement."

— Survey respondent

We must not ignore the wise counsel of our spouses. We must listen to the concerns and questions of our children. If your family and your dream are at odds, pass a magnifying glass over your life. Consider the wisdom of Proverbs 11:29:

The one who brings ruin on his household
will inherit the wind,
and a fool will be a slave
to someone whose heart is wise.

When the disciples were called, some of them were commanded to leave their families. What's not apparent is how God provided for these loved ones in the absence of the husbands and fathers that followed the Lord Jesus. I believe he provided for his loved ones at home through relatives, other believers, or supernatural means.

God does not change nor contradict himself. The truths about providing for your family are clear in Scripture. In fact, the following verse may clarify a dilemma that you and your spouse are grappling with: "Now if anyone does not provide for his own relatives, and especially for his household, he has denied the faith and is worse than an unbeliever" (1 Tim. 5:8).

If you leave your job and follow a low-paying ministry path, are you *really* obeying God's commands to lead, manage, provide for, and serve your family? This is a clear obligation detailed in Scripture. Only you can answer what *provision* means for your family.

Through your journey into ministry, God may want to adjust your family's concept of *wants* versus *needs*. A ministry-supported lifestyle may be exactly what God has in mind to teach lessons about materialism, faith, or trust in him. After all, you can't serve both God and money—but God *did* give us money as a tool to meet our family's needs and enable ministry in the world.

I am not precluding God's prerogative to lift you out of the life you know to do his bidding. But you must hear the Lord's voice clearly and have no doubt that you are to relinquish your family obligations. He gives us strong commands to provide for our families. Neglecting them because you *want* to go into ministry is dangerous and will destroy your effectiveness as a pastor or missionary or any type of leader.

The disciples were chosen to literally follow Jesus as he walked past them. Our lesson is to follow him too, but only out of obedience. In the book of Luke, two men volunteered their services to Jesus but were not accepted. They had their own desire to follow the Lord, rather than a divine invitation to join his earthly ministry. The Lord rejected them both: "As they were traveling on the road someone said to Him, 'I will follow You wherever You go!' Jesus told him, 'Foxes have dens, and birds of the sky have nests, but the Son of Man has no place to lay His head.' . . . Another also said, 'I will follow You, Lord, but first let me go and say good-bye to those at my house.' But Jesus said to him, 'No one who puts his hand to the plow and looks back is fit for the kingdom of God'" (Luke 9: 57–58, 61–62).

Between these two men who approached Jesus of their own volition, there was another whom Jesus singled out with a distinct invitation. The man apparently was minding his own business, unprepared for the Lord's command: "Then He said to another, 'Follow Me.' 'Lord,' he said, 'first let me go bury my father.' But He told him, 'Let the dead bury their own dead, but you go and spread the news of the kingdom of God'" (Luke 9:59–60).

If the Lord points at you and beckons like that, even your father's funeral shouldn't get in the way of following the Lord right at that moment.

The point is, when the Lord pulls you into ministry, he will make sure the needs of you and your family are met. If you are forcing the issue—volunteering your services out of pride or personal desire rather than following out of obedience—be prepared for rejection. But remember, "rejection" may actually mean "not now"—a temporary pause in the action. In the Lord's perfect timing, you may be feeling a draw that is not yet a call. He may have other lessons for you to learn, other plans for your family. The pieces may not be in place just yet.

STEP 5: EXPLORE YOUR LAND OF OPPORTUNITY—AND THE COST

If you've spent much time in the marketplace, you know how crucial planning is to the success of any venture. Blindly stepping into the future is a death wish for your business. If a company's executives don't keep their eyes on the months ahead, personnel surprises, competition, unpredictable cash flow, or other market forces can knock the organization around like a sailboat in a typhoon until "business as usual" becomes "out of business."

Planning, forecasting, budgeting, and market research are necessary ingredients for any thriving business. So too are long-term vision and goals to achieve along the way.

EXPLORING THE PROMISED LAND

Though the Lord led his people to a land destined to be their home for current and future generations, he first directed Moses to send in spies to check out the soil, the strength and number of the inhabitants and their cities, and the quality of the trees and fruit.

The spies reported that the land did indeed flow with milk and honey, but the people were giants, the cities large and fortified. The Israelites shamed God by believing those obstacles were greater than he, and he passed judgment on them by preventing virtually an entire generation from entering. They failed the test of faith.

I wonder if God would ever choose to show me all the obstacles in my future, and if so, would I shy away from his will or believe that he would glorify himself by overcoming those difficulties?

As you look at a future of financial difficulty, persecution, loss of status, or emotional pain, does your faith well up in you like a mighty sword to slash through the obstacles? Do you believe in your soul that the Lord will set your feet on solid ground?

Or do you see a mountain too steep to climb?

"Apply your business understanding and expectations to the organization you're going to join, because even though it is a nonprofit, what frustrates you about your current job will most likely frustrate you about your ministry position."　　　　　　　　　　—Survey respondent

When you scout out your own promised land, you can bet there will be giants *and* luscious fruit. Our most valuable lessons are found in pain, our greatest growth in overcoming challenges. But follow the example set by Moses: look before you leap. Search out the plan God is laying out for you. Know where you're going so you know how best to serve God and his church.

Moses said, "Then all of you approached me and said, 'Let's send men ahead of us, so that they may explore the land for us and bring us back a report about *the route we should go up and the cities we will come to*'" (Deut. 1:22, my emphasis).

You should know the best path to your destination and where the milestones and goals are along the way. Every journey has rest areas and short-term destinations. Moses saw wisdom in knowing ahead of time what to expect on the journey, discovering what specific towns would be in their path. He saw no wisdom in blindly walking into the land, even though it had been promised by the Lord.

If you've confirmed your calling, it's time to scout out the land and its inhabitants.

COUNTING THE SPIRITUAL COST

Luke 14 expands on the wisdom of scouting out your opportunity. Here we learn to count the cost of following the Lord's calling. He paints in vivid color what he requires from his disciples.

"Check out the infrastructure of the church leadership. Find out who serves on the board of directors. How does the senior pastor view business skills? Are these skills respected as necessary to the job, as much as the praise and worship leader must be able to sing?"

—Survey respondent

Jesus says anyone who is not willing to hate his wife, parents, and children is not fit to be a disciple. But how can we forsake our family, when the Bible also says if we don't provide for them, we are worse than an unbeliever (1 Tim. 5:8)?

In his supporting analogy, Jesus speaks the language of the marketplace: "For which of you, wanting to build a tower, doesn't first sit down and calculate the cost to see if he has enough to complete it? Otherwise, after he has laid the foundation and cannot finish it, all the onlookers will begin to make fun of him, saying, 'This man started to build and wasn't able to finish'" (Luke 14:28–30).

Jesus teaches that we need to understand the full cost of service to him. We must be willing to lay down everything and everyone we love. When we identify every obstacle and comfort in our lives that may prevent effective service to him and give them up, we can fully identify as his disciple.

In God's perfection, he spurned his own Son for our sake so that we might live. He allowed his Son to die. He identified with us, teaching through his example that our lives are not our own. Our ultimate expression of love and obedience to this gracious Father is to surrender our own lives and be willing to turn from our family as he turned from his.

When we are willing to give up every ounce of our will to trust him with our most precious earthly treasures, he can take our surrendered hearts to new heights. Our weakness and broken heart awaken the power of the Holy Spirit in our walk. If I offer the family that I love more than my own life, I am in my most vulnerable, broken, dependent state. I would be nothing without them.

And yet Jesus wants me to trust that *he* will provide for them, *he* will protect them, *he* will save them.

In this parable of examining the requirements of erecting a tower, we discover a rich lesson. Christ exhorts us to calculate the cost of our commitment to him. He admonishes us to plan for the coming sacrifices and trust him for the inevitable surprises. Wisdom is knowing what we're getting into—not blindly dropping off a precipice of opportunity, grasping for a helping hand.

Are you willing to pay the price of following your Lord? He desires a sacrifice at your core. He yearns for you to trust him with your valuables.

When you are willing to pay whatever the Lord requires in your innermost heart, he will remind you of the price he already paid. His best for your family won't be far behind.

I can't end this section without encouragement from Paul. Because most of the other disciples, including Jesus's own brothers, brought their wives and children with them on their journeys, they were under the "maintenance" of the church, which meant their food and drink and all other basic needs were supplied by the churches they visited. Paul asks in 1 Corinthians 9:11, "If we have sown spiritual things for you, is it too much if we reap material things from you?" The disciples and their families had the right to receive support from other believers.

While the Lord wants you to lay everything of value at his feet, including your beloved family, he has shown that he fuses them back to you with an even stronger bond. You do not labor alone. You and your spouse are one flesh.

Read Paul's defense of the rights of the apostles: "Don't we have the right to be accompanied by a Christian wife, like the other apostles, the Lord's brothers, and Cephas?" (1 Cor. 9:5).

Cephas (the apostle Peter) was a family man in full-time ministry. He did not forsake his family responsibilities, nor did he embrace celibacy. His wife accompanied him. Christ's own brothers—James, Joseph, Simon, and Judas—took wives and served in ministry.

Family-oriented mission work abounded as more disciples responded to the call—and what a training ground for children! Can you imagine seeing your father preach to strangers, suffer persecution, lead hundreds to Christ, drive out demons, perform miracles, and defend the faith against malicious mobs? What would that do to your own spiritual growth? The effects of such leadership by example would raise up another generation of faithful warriors and godly women.

Talk to your family. Pray for your family. Offer them to the Lord. If you are answering God's commission to devote your worklife to the ministry, he can turn their hearts to you.

And how much easier your work will be.

STEP 6: SCRUTINIZE YOUR EDUCATIONAL QUALIFICATIONS

None of us are born theological or business geniuses. We may inherit an affinity for learning or an especially good memory, but the source of our smarts is a mixture of our upbringing, schooling, passions, experience, interests, and hard knocks.

When you step into a ministry role, the skills and knowledge you developed over your lifetime may suddenly lack one necessary ingredient: seminary training. Not all ministry careers require a theological degree, but entering into ministry without a solid foundation or the right qualifications can hurt those you serve. Don't forget that you're held to a higher standard by the Lord when you're a pastor or teacher of the Word. If you have any doubt about your qualifications, you must prepare and train to "correctly [teach] the word of truth" (2 Tim. 2:15).

If your desired ministry work will clearly benefit from further education—and it will almost every time—the sooner you dive in, the better, according to one of the leaders in our study: "Consider getting some kind of education, even if it is only a few online courses. You must be well grounded in the Word, even if you plan to be in a support-only role."

Another says, "Complete your education while you're still working." The key to a smooth transition—especially when your finances and education need time to work out—is to hold on to your current job as long as possible. Going to school costs money. Prematurely quitting your job costs even more.

Finding the right seminary requires hours of research. Hundreds of "distance learning" Web sites beckon with opportunities. But don't choose a school based on mere words and pictures on the screen. Visit one or two seminaries and talk to current and former students, professors, and staff. Don't pass up the chance to enhance your learning in an interactive face-to-face setting.

And remember to figure your family into the education equation. "Make sure your family is first after God," says one respondent. "School and ministry work should *never* come before your family. If it takes three times as long to get through school, take that road, rather than never seeing your family."

STEP 7: MAKE AN INFORMED DECISION ON YOUR FUTURE

Use the following checklist as you confirm your decision.

Make it realistic. Realize that you're in for a whole new set of troubles that come with ministry and the possibility of reduced income. Review the next chapter on financial planning.

"Don't have high career expectations. Plan on serving God and God's people without any ego gratification. It will be hard, sometimes painful work with few (if any) tangible rewards. The rewards will be spiritual and emotional, but sometimes that may not be enough."

—Survey respondent

Make it according to your vision. Take your vision statement seriously. It should be a succinct picture of your future and should drive your plan. It may be a good idea to write it on a note card and tape it to the side of your computer screen or your bathroom mirror.

Don't make it in a vacuum. Don't trust your own intelligence, instincts, or inquiries to give you all the information you need. Take a risk and open yourself up to other opinions. You're better off getting tough questions from trusted friends now than dragging your family through a field of suffering later. Ask God to open his thoughts and intentions to you.

> "For My thoughts are not your thoughts,
> and your ways are not My ways."
> [This is] the LORD's declaration.
> "For as heaven is higher than earth,
> so My ways are higher than your ways,
> and My thoughts than your thoughts." (Isa. 55:8–9)

Make it as soon as possible. Souls are at risk, my friend. The sooner you get about the business of ministry, the more people you can impact for eternity.

Make it public. You should be proud of your decision to serve the Lord full-time. Write letters to advisors to announce your plans. Fire off an e-mail to your pastor. Seek out close friends to let them in on your decision. After your boss or partner is aware, take your colleagues to lunch to tell them the good news. Some will be happy for you, others will be jealous, and a few will call you foolish. Paul became a fool on purpose when he quit his "government" job, so you'll be in good company.

Make it long-term. Expect many years of hard work, few earthly rewards, and moments of doubt. But what you endure and accomplish on earth will determine your reward in heaven. Just imagine what your trove of heavenly treasure might look like after a lifetime of serving the Lord.

STEP 8: TRUST THE LORD— AND LOOK FOR CONFIRMATION

I am an impatient man. I have also been known to worry when a bad situation lasts longer than I prefer. I'm anxious for change, improvement, and turnaround.

Therefore God directs me to read the book of Psalms. Whenever I turn to those poetic pages, I feel God's hand on my shoulder and hear his soft voice. "I'm right here," he says. "I haven't forgotten you. I've got it under control. You can let go of your worry now."

The following verse exemplifies the comfort I receive from this book: "Wait for the LORD; / be courageous and let your heart be strong. / Wait for the LORD" (Ps. 27:14).

In his classic devotional *My Utmost for His Highest*, Oswald Chambers writes about heavenly patience: "When it is a question of the providential will of God, wait for God to move." This reminds us who is in charge of our decisions.

"I owned a consulting business. In the process of selling it, I was required to sign a one-year contract [to stay] involved in the company to ensure the transition of clients.

"I went to seminary part-time during that window. Everything else pretty much fell into place. Home sold, wife was offered a one-year package to retire from an ailing corporate oil company.

"It was an exciting confirmation."   —Survey respondent

If, in your crossover ministry planning, you decide something must happen before you can take the next step—whether you must achieve debt-free status, heal a family relationship, or get a car so you can get to class—lift it up to the Lord. Wait for his hand to move. When he does, praise him for his confirmation. When a necessary element of the transition is out of your control or power to accomplish, pray that the Lord will step in and take care of it. Then wait.

STEP 9: DON'T LOOK BACK

When you break out of the gate to chase your vision, run like a Kentucky Derby horse. Have you ever seen one of those muscular, determined animals look back? Never. Their necks

---

"If you commit to the calling, commit with all you have—no holding back—for God, the flesh, and the devil will all work to test you, and quitting is not an option. Ministry is **not** a Sunday school class."

—Survey respondent

---

stretch forward. Their eyes focus on the next turn, the horse in front of them, or the paddock beyond the finish line.

Like that racehorse, when you know your mission and have been released to pursue it, you should pant and strain until a hand from above loosens the reins or you cross the finish line.

Another research respondent advises that you talk to ministers about their joys and frustrations. Find out what, if anything, brings them down. Listen to their personal struggles. Hear how they draw encouragement from friends or congregants. "It helps when you face those same frustrations to know they're normal," says another crossover leader, "and it helps to keep you from looking back and thinking you left a good thing in the business world."

POINTS TO PONDER

1. Have you prayed earnestly and often about your plans?
2. Is your family behind your decision?
3. What concrete confirmation has God given you to pursue a ministry career?
4. Has he given you a personal vision?

4
IIIIIIIIIIIII

The Faith/Planning Paradox: Overcoming the Financial Goliath

Churches are noted for bad pay.
—SURVEY RESPONDENT

I struggle with something—maybe you do too. I don't always know how to balance faith in the Lord's will with the biblical admonition to plan and prepare.

Many Christians "let the Spirit move" and act spontaneously in any given situation, while others believe we should ask God for guidance in our planning.

Recently my church's minister used a short illustration that gave me perspective on this paradox.

Our large church, he said, couldn't offer enough child care, Sunday school classes, communion cups and wafers, quality music, or dozens of clean bathrooms without the huge organization of workers behind the scenes. Not only are there more than three hundred staff members, but thousands of volunteers ensure a level of excellence in every aspect of the church, from the flow of traffic in the parking lot to high-quality articles in the church paper.

Then he told a story about Martin Luther, the father of Protestantism. Apparently this Christian giant wrestled with the faith/planning contradiction himself.

One day Martin Luther waited for a message from the Lord for his sermon. He wanted to give the Spirit room to move without the hindrance of his own human intervention. He prepared nothing. He trusted that God would speak through him—the right words at the right time.

When Luther walked up to the pulpit, God indeed spoke in his ear: "Martin Luther, you are not prepared."

In this chapter we will explore this paradox of faith and planning as you consider your transition into ministry.

The following questions may be on your mind as you create your own plan: If I plan too much, am I distrusting God's promise of provision? If I decide to go only on faith and trust, am I disobeying the Lord's command to plan wisely?

When Jesus implores us to count the cost of following him, we rarely think about the financial side of the equation. *If God calls me,* you might think, *he'll take care of all my needs.* This is what happened for most of the leaders in our study—they trusted and God provided.

For others, the faith factor became a stumbling block. "I had just gotten my family to a place where we were making some good money," notes one respondent, when the financial realities of his new life set in, raising blinders in front of his ministry vision. Financial pressures affected another leader's family relationships: "My wife had to leave a beautiful home and a good lifestyle to one where she had to go back to work, and all of our savings disappeared. My daughter was a senior in high school and the financial support for her college education was gone. This caused a major wall in our relationship."

Are there keys to dealing with the financial obstacle? Most crossover leaders in the study admitted they struggled with meeting material needs during all stages of ministry, but especially during seminary and the early years. In some cases, providing for their families while pursuing ministry led to doubt, fatigue, and hardship.

"My wife was the only wage earner. . . . At times we didn't have food. Those were very lean years, but God always provided at what seemed to be the last moment. I wouldn't trade those years for anything. They forged the trust and obedience we needed to survive ministry and helped us relate to those we minister to who have even less than we did!"

—Survey respondent

However difficult the financial transition, these leaders want to give you encouragement. One comment summarizes it well: "I have not missed a meal or been rained on."

KEYS TO BALANCING THE PARADOX

This chapter doesn't promise a "three-step plan to financial independence" before you go into ministry. Your situation is unique and only the Lord knows all the circumstances and variables heaped on you now. But I propose three strategies that have helped leaders cross into ministry with more solid financial footing. I'll also reveal the regrets of those who mishandled their own finances. And along the way we will try to grasp a balanced perspective on the financial faith/planning paradox.

God has given each of us a certain measure of faith with which to navigate life's twisting road. We can spend hours planning and researching the future paths of our lives, but we shouldn't trust in our human striving: "For by the grace given to me, I tell everyone among you not to think of himself more highly than he should think. Instead, think sensibly, as God has distributed a measure of faith to each one" (Rom. 12:3).

If we don't think sensibly about our schemes, we may be ignoring obvious realities. I tend to dream about alternative futures and sometimes get irritated when I have to deal with a daily to-do list of "menial" tasks. While I love "visioneering," sober reality anchors me in the now. Bills stack up. Meetings must be attended. Relationships require nurturing and effort. Minute by minute, new realities poke through the daydream cloud. My feet must drop back to the floor.

Don't be ashamed of your concern for your family's finances in light of your ministry calling. Planning your financial transition is an act of obedience. You honor the Lord when you work hard to provide for your family. Throwing them to the wind as you chase after your calling is in direct conflict to God's commands (remember 1 Timothy 5:8—he who doesn't provide for his family is "worse than an unbeliever.") And without a wise, thought-out financial strategy, you may be ignoring the Lord's wisdom in truly "counting the cost of following him." Faith and planning may seem like opposites, but they actually feed off each other in perfect harmony.

Seek God's Wisdom and Plan First

Remember, the Lord has already drafted a plan for your life's work—it's your job to discover it. When I fear I'm messing up his perfect plan, I'm soon reminded that I'm a mere speck in the grand design of our Lord and Creator: "A man's heart plans his way, / but the LORD determines his steps" (Prov. 16:9).

This encouraging verse is my license for faith. No matter how far off base my plan, God will make sure my feet stay on the path he's charted. How wonderful to know I can't step into a hole without the Lord already knowing how he'll rescue me.

At one of Church Central's consultant training conferences I met Scott Jefferson, a mild-mannered man whose eyes sparkle with intelligence and compassion. Over lunch we talked about what brought him to Louisville to learn how to consult with churches. His business-to-ministry testimony caused the others at our table to share their stories. When I learned that three out of my four tablemates had left the business world for ministry, I suspected it was an anomaly. But of the fifty total attendees, more than a third reported similar journeys.

Scott's life story sparked my passion to learn more about this interesting crowd. His account will supercharge your faith and enlighten your financial perspective. Allow me to introduce you to him.

LIFESTORY

Scott Jefferson—
From Top Corporate Exec to Pastor
Age at crossover: 48
Former position: VP Human Resources/Legal Affairs
Company: Morton Salt
Key quote: "The purpose of my life was ministry, not money."

Scott Jefferson flew the company plane twice a year to the Bahamas on business. He drew a six-figure income plus bonuses and stock options. Working as vice president of human resources and legal affairs for Morton Salt International Inc., he was responsible for ten thousand employees in seven countries and all over the United States.

But Scott recalls the day everything changed. The company president applauded him for his performance—something that should have encouraged him to continue his hard work. Instead, it nudged him further toward something he had been considering for more than twenty years, and he tendered his resignation.

"He said something like, if I had stayed with the company, I'd one day be rich," Scott recalls of the good performance review. But he had known for a long time that being rich was not his ultimate aim.

In a sense, Scott was never a businessman at heart. He was a minister. Even studying business, receiving a master's degree in finance, and then pursuing a law degree, he knew he was a minister.

He accepted Christ at fifteen, influenced by the faith of his mother. Then as a college student, he recommitted his life to Christ and began to evangelize on campus. "I have never stopped since that point," he says.

He was ordained in the Church of God in Christ in 1978 and worked in ministry with a mentoring pastor while he was still in school. "At the time I was studying law, I already knew what my calling was ultimately—full-time ministry." But he entered the business world nonetheless.

Scott says his calling didn't fade, even through years of work in the corporate world. "Scripture talks about wearing this world as a loose-fitting garment," he says. "In the back of my mind I always remembered that ministry was my primary purpose."

He says he was waiting for his calling, for the right time and place God would use him in ministry. "I knew that it was God's timing and that it was God's will for me," he says.

While working for Morton, Scott started a church in 1989 with three families meeting in his living room. Ten years later the call came to quit his day job and minister full-time.

Then, even though he had been prepared for it, expected it, and waited for it for years, he struggled with his faith and God's will.

"I tried to bargain with God. I said, 'OK, God, if you want me to go into the ministry, you bless me.'"

God asked him to take a step of faith. The blessing was to come after the commitment. "God said, 'No, if you go into the ministry, I'll bless you.'"

Already Scott was making more money than he thought he could ever make, more money than he could spend—so much that paying for four daughters' college tuition was not even a concern for him in the career move.

"The Holy Spirit put an impression on my heart," he says. "The purpose of my life was ministry, not money."

So he leapt. "I went from the pinnacle of corporate America to servanthood."

The living room church had been growing and continued to grow. Today True Light Fellowship Ministries in Dyer, Indiana, is building a new facility to accommodate one thousand worshippers.

The growth didn't surprise Scott. He believed God would be faithful to his ministry. What did surprise him was how busy ministry was. Before becoming a full-time pastor, the then forty-eight-year-old executive was concerned he wouldn't be challenged enough in ministry.

He would no longer have the challenge of constantly being confronted with legal situations, employment concerns, mergers and acquisitions, due diligence, and lawsuits. He would no longer have "10,000 people calling . . . with 10,000 questions." And he would in essence be giving up his law practice.

"I didn't know how I would handle going from all of that activity to just ministry," he says. "But ministry has filled the void very well. As a matter of fact, I make the joke that I left my part-time job to go to my full-time job."

As a minister Scott has been able to use some of his negotiating skills and his understanding of business principles. He still uses his legal skills for churches that need his help in incorporation or property issues. He does some pro bono work but also works as a certified church consultant for churches in need.

Looking back, Scott realizes that "God has a progression for all of us. Sometimes the most difficult thing is to go through that progression."

But, he says, the most important part of the decision to move from business to ministry was the prayer that surrounded it. For others considering a similar move, Scott says, "Pray. Pray diligently and know that it is God. Don't do it on a whim. Don't do it because someone else is doing it or because of what you think is going to happen. Pray. Seek counsel from someone senior in the ministry that you respect and admire. Then after you've done all that and you know that it is God— go for it."

THREE KEYS TO FINANCIAL FAITH

It may surprise you, but not everyone who leaves the marketplace will be able to pay for four college tuitions. So what do we do when the calling is sure, but the finances aren't in place yet? If your future seems a little less stable, I pray the following three keys will help unlock the foundation of your financial plan.

KEY 1: SEEK FIRST THE KINGDOM— AND WISDOM—OF GOD

King Solomon, the wisest man in history, had a perspective on life similar to Scott Jefferson's. When the time came to serve, money held no sway over this godly king. He simply wanted to live up to the task assigned to him, which was to govern the Lord's people. The following account of Solomon's conversation with God illustrates how a faithful search for heavenly wisdom was blessed with much more than the knowledge he sought.

> That night God appeared to Solomon and said to him: "Ask. What should I give you?"
>
> And Solomon said to God: "You have shown great faithful love to my father David, and You have made me king in his place. LORD God, let your promise to my father David now come true. For you have made me king over a people as numerous as the dust of the earth. Now, grant me wisdom and knowledge so that I may lead this people, for who can judge this great people of yours?"
>
> God said to Solomon, "Because this was in your heart, and you have not requested riches, wealth, or glory, or for the life of those who hate you, and

you have not even requested long life, but you have requested for yourself wisdom and knowledge that you may judge my people over whom I have made you king, wisdom and knowledge are given to you. I will also give you riches, wealth, and glory, such that it was not like this for the kings who were before you, nor will it be like this for those after you." (2 Chron. 1:7–12)

The Lord rewarded Solomon's pure heart with his true desire: wisdom to carry out his calling. I believe a litmus test to determine the purity of our own heart lies in a single question: am I passionately obedient to the Lord's call? I can't focus first on my personal needs. That comes after I surrender in obedience to whatever the Lord may ask me to do.

A couple of years ago, our oldest son Matt asked three rapid-fire questions before he bounced from the bed to the floor in the mornings: "What are we having for breakfast? Can I have something on my shirt? Are we having company today?"

After my wife divulged the menu and picked out a shirt with a football or bulldozer design for him and his two-year-old brother, she would say, "Well, I haven't invited anyone to come over, but you never know what God might have in store!"

If her mom popped in unexpectedly with lunch or a friend dropped by unannounced between errands, Karen and the boys got a kick out of God's surprise guests. The lesson she was teaching our little guys was that while we may make our own plans in life, God is ultimately in control and will surprise us along the way.

When we seek the Lord's will and ask for wisdom in our planning, we should always expect—and leave room for—those surprise guests that will surely drop in at any time.

KEY 2: TRUST THE LORD FOR YOUR NEEDS

As you look at your financial future, can you even now trust your material needs to the Lord? Do you have faith that God has your best interests at heart, even if your plan falls apart or some of those surprise guests do some damage? Consider the obstacle-turned-blessing in this crossover leader's story: "God took care of one of the greatest obstacles by allowing me to lose my job due to downsizing. . . . There is much more to the story, but just let me say that God provided even more than I could ever have imagined. Due to losing my job, I was able to attend seminary through job rehab training, which relieved a financial burden from my family."

Some crossover leaders like Scott Jefferson told us their faith in God's provision during their business years was too easy. Their paycheck delivered itself every two weeks, their retirement account grew without much thought, their health benefits silently hovered in the wings. The future took care of itself. After evolving into ministry, however, when those things suddenly lost their regularity—or disappeared altogether— the leaders had no choice but to trust. This new level of faith sprouted out of necessity and matured with time.

We honor God when we trust him. A few years ago he stretched my own faith when a business venture I had co-founded started swirling down the drain. My intense fear threw me into a depression. When I was ready to listen, the Lord assured me he had it under control. It took time, but finally the venture staged a massive turnaround and is very stable today. In the process of waiting, I read the Bible more, praying and relying on him—exactly what he wanted in the first place.

KEY 3: PREPARE FOR THE COMING FINANCIAL STRUGGLE

Unless your bank account suddenly swells from an inheritance or you have a sizable savings built up, you will probably butt up against a wall of financial challenges before or during your ministry. Financial obstacles reared up time and again in our research. Some leaders regretted not planning better for their families. Others received more blessings than they expected.

Wherever you land in your view of faith and planning, Jesus said, "You will have suffering in this world" (John 16:33). Therefore, even if you have the greatest faith *and* craft the ultimate no-fail plan, you will still encounter difficulty. In his simple statement, Jesus implores us to rely on faith more than human planning and striving.

Then how do we rectify this faith with "counting the cost"? Does Christ command us to count the cost, have faith, *and* expect trouble all at the same time?

Of course he does. These three mind-sets are not mutually exclusive. We are to provide for our families and ourselves. We are to trust in the Lord with all our hearts (Prov. 3:5). We are to stand against the Devil's tactics (Eph. 6:11). And when we ask for God's help in these three areas, trusting that he will provide and protect, we grow in our knowledge and trust of him because of our increased prayer and Bible reading.

In the following pages, a couple of stories illustrate how two men transitioned into ministry while God showed them how he would provide.

LIFESTORY

Mark Carden—
From Accountant
to Executive Pastor
Age at crossover: 37
Former position: Business Assurance Partner
Company: PriceWaterhouseCoopers
Key quote: "I am reminded every day ... that there is nothing more exciting or satisfying than doing what God wants you to do."

"I graduated in 1981 with a bachelor's in accounting from Texas A&M then worked for a Big Eight firm known today as PriceWaterhouseCoopers. I married my high school sweetheart, Lisa, in May 1982. We have three wonderful children.

"In July 1991, I was selected to be a Practice Fellow at the Financial Accounting Standards Board (a great honor!). After returning to Houston in July 1993, I was admitted to the Partnership of Coopers & Lybrand. Within a couple months we received a request for a proposal from a large company that had just bought my largest client. In early 1994, we won the engagement and I moved my family to New Orleans to work on the account. In early 1995, I was named the audit leader of our U.S. utility practice. Life was great and I was making more money than I ever thought I could. And I loved my job.

"Then, in August 1995, we returned to Houston on vacation. During that trip my best friend asked me if I would consider moving back and serving with him as the executive pastor of his church. My first reaction was negative, but I began praying about it. About a month later, I read the book

Halftime (by Bob Buford), which made me reconsider. Then Lisa and I attended a Christian business conference where it seemed every speaker was speaking directly to me about this decision.

"After praying constantly and seeking counsel from mentors, friends, and family, God convinced me and Lisa this was what he wanted me to do. In November 1995 I committed to the pastorate, and then God started showing me how he would take care of me.

"I informed the managing partner in the firm about my decision, and he offered me a part-time role in the audit practice. This worked out perfectly, because this new church couldn't afford for me to be full-time yet, plus I wasn't sure *I* could afford to be a full-time pastor right away. On May 1, 1996, I began working half-time in the practice and half-time as the executive pastor of this two-year-old, 330-member church. I continued that dual role until the end of 1999, when the church grew enough to take me on full-time.

"I am reminded every day I wake up that there is nothing more exciting or satisfying than doing what God wants you to do. Serving in a church of 3,500 people that is leading the unchurched to become fully devoted followers of Jesus Christ is a great joy and blessing in my life. I am forever grateful for this opportunity to serve."

Six Steps to Building Your Family's Financial Plan

Bob Buford in *Halftime* says most midpoint lifers who want to shift their careers enter a transition time where they work in the marketplace and ministry until finances or other circumstances fall into place. Another reason they split their careers for awhile is to confirm that this specific ministry is where God wants them. So there's a new meaning for *half-time*—dividing your *work time* in half.

As you flesh out the material needs and money side of your ministry plan, the following six steps should help you develop a sound, downsized financial strategy.

1. Create a budget. This step may seem obvious, but it's surprising how many people ignore it to their detriment. While I've always handled the finances in our family, I admit I've adhered to a strict budget only in the past few years. A simple budget has made a huge difference because I know exactly how much I have to spend, to put in savings, to sock away for Christmas, and to tithe. It allows us to live within our means and not get broadsided every month by little surprises that send us into the negative realm in our checkbook (which I've allowed to happen too many times).

Any spreadsheet software like Excel will let you make a budget. You simply list all your spending categories on the left, your income on the top, and record actual spending next to the respective budgeted amounts every month. I've included the Harper family budget below (with fictitious amounts) to illustrate one way to keep track of your money. I recommend you go to the bookstore or browse Web sites that can help you learn more advanced budgeting (Larry Burkett's Crown Financial Ministries is an excellent resource—go to www.crown.org for useful information and an online budget calculator).

I decided to forego the fancy programs and templates and manually record everything I knew our family spent money on. It took me a few months to get it all down accurately. I entered our actual expenses and started comparing the "money in" and "money out" totals every month. This helped me control expenditures like big gifts, extravagant dinners, or uncontrollable splurges at the bookstore.

2006 Budget	Jan. Budgeted	Jan. Actual
Tithe/gift	$325	$325
Car payment	$278	$278
Babysitting	$75	$24
Cable	$47	$47
Phone and Internet	$100	$129
Cell phone	$45	$109
Christmas savings	$100	$100
Cleaners	$85	$80
Clothes	$75	$50
Credit card debt	$100	$100
Dinner and lunch out	$225	$200
Entertainment and books	$75	$83
Gas and repairs	$70	$85
Gifts/toys	$50	$40
Grocery and drug items	$800	$823
Home improvement	$75	$72
Home security	$33	$33
Insurance—car and house	$138	$138
Louisville Gas & Electric	$130	$190
Medical expenses	$75	$50
Mortgage	$800	$800
Savings	$100	$100
Vacation	$100	$100
Waste pickup	$28	$28
Water	$120	$120
Miscellaneous and school	$100	$100
TOTAL EXPENDITURES	$4,149	$4,204

Did you notice that some estimates in the first column don't match their actual expenses? Don't expect real life to match your budget. Your goal is to get close to your estimates and keep your spending under control. I went a little over for the month. Other months will be slightly under. It's important to set aside regular installments for the big seasonal or one-time expenses like vacations, Christmas gifts, medical needs, and unexpected car repairs.

If this were my actual budget for my current job, and a ministry opportunity I was considering was only going to pay me $2,500 a month, I'd have to make drastic cuts to work within my new salary, or I'd split my time between a secular job and the church for awhile. Some crossover leaders in our research admitted it took longer than they thought to reach a comfort level with their new lower income.

No matter your accounting expertise, you *must* create a budget so you can steward the money and other resources God gives you. You can't completely count the cost without seeing these numbers and wisely adjusting your expenditures to suit God's direction. Before you leap over the career fence, create a hypothetical budget to see what life will be like on much less salary.

2. *Don't touch your retirement account.* It's there for emergencies, unexpected expenses, living costs when you retire or can no longer work, vacations, second-childhood toys, and—if there's some left—for your children or charities when you're gone. If you don't have any retirement savings, you, my friend, need to put this book down and get started or you could face a financial crisis later in life.

"Retirement is for wimps," I recently heard a baby boomer say. And many baby boomers entering retirement age now are planning to work longer—possibly the rest of their physically or mentally able years. But what if those years are cut short because of illness or disaster, and the expenses continue to mount? I, for one, wouldn't want my children or other family members to feel a financial burden because of me. Remember, Paul manufactured and sold tents so he wouldn't be a burden on the church's finances.

Therefore I recommend you not only keep your retirement fund intact but continue to build it through your ministry years. Getting a job at a church should not mean you throw future financial security out the window. Though you may sacrifice many material possessions to enter the ministry, fiercely protect your retirement nest egg. And don't use it to pay bills.

3. Plan on keeping some kind of job during the ministry transition. While you go back to school and during the first few years of full-time ministry, don't automatically drop your day job. The Lord may indeed want you in ministry full-time, right away. He alone controls your destiny and your finances. If you have tested your calling against Scripture, counted the cost, and sense your path has been confirmed by the Lord, you must obey indeed.

But if you're still investigating your calling or haven't fully counted the cost yet, there's one more thing to think about. Since God has given you certain talents and skills to earn money, he may want you to continue to use them to meet your daily needs while your ministry develops. Our respondents employed this strategy often. It made sense for them. It was confirmed in their circumstances and in the various provisions that God brought at just the right time.

"It may not have to be an all-or-nothing decision. You may be able to fulfill the call of God and continue your secular employment."

—Survey respondent

---

4. Look closely at your home. Contrary to popular wisdom, your dwelling is not your greatest asset but your greatest monthly expense. Unless you already live in modest quarters, bear in mind the money you could save every month if you downsized.

Consider how much equity you have and if it could be used for a sizable down payment on a smaller house or condo. Don't rent an apartment—if you're going to shell out bucks every month for your four walls, at least put your money toward ownership. Then you'll have another potential down payment for a future move.

5. Get outside support for your schooling. We've already discussed the importance of seminary or additional training. There's no reason to deplete your family's personal funds for it, especially when you're already preparing for less income long-term. You have options, including applying for a scholarship, finding personal donors, or appealing to your church for help.

6. Carefully plan your transition out of your job. The paradox of faith and planning can be unclear at times for marketplace leaders who are used to being organized, budgeted, and strategized. Remember Martin Luther: though he thought he would wait for the Spirit to move, God rebuked him for not preparing his sermon. Throughout Scripture we are admonished to count the cost, to ask for wisdom and knowledge, and to trust the Lord with all our hearts.

If you seek the Lord's wisdom, trust him for your needs, and prepare for a possible financial struggle, you don't have to choose faith or planning. The Lord wants us to pray for guidance as we plan our future according to the call we have received. Then we trust that God will provide for our families and bless our efforts. We are to faithfully plan . . . and the Lord will be faithful to his promises.

"The company I am working for has repeatedly [tried] to promote/transfer me to positions that would derail my ministry goals. Climbing the ladder at my company would seriously hamper my opportunities for ministry."

"My parents took the decision hard because they expected me to take over the family business."

"I had emotional trauma from leaving a position of prestige and influence where I was respected in the business community to waking up one day at age forty and being a nobody trying to learn Greek verbs."

—Survey respondents

Let me introduce you to a man who experienced hardship beyond imagining, whose radical career transition stands out among all my interviews and research.

LifeStory

Skip Moen, PhD—
From Multimillionaire
to Victim of Devastating Fraud
Age at crossover: 48
Former position: CEO
Company: Human resources consulting firm
Key quote: "There are times when I miss the Ferrari and the parties and the trips."

"At forty-eight, I had virtually every material thing and I planned on never working again.

"But as I look back on my past, I see that I have been like Moses, living a hidden life in the desert. My forty years came to an end in a dramatic and unnerving way, just as Moses' forty years ended when he encountered God in the burning bush. Moses hid from the world on the back side of the desert. I hid from the world (and from God) by living in a desert inside my soul.

"In spite of the trappings of success, every day I struggled with the fear that I might be exposed for who I really was. I came to believe that I was unacceptable to God. I feared his punishment. He was my moral accountant, keeping track of all the sins on my record. I tried to run from God.

"My desert life brought me years of pain, and I became a man without fire. I sought relief in what pleasures could be found in the desert. They were only temporary reprieves at best. They usually drove me deeper and deeper into the wasteland.

"I don't know why God decided that it was time for a burning bush in my life. I'll get to ask him someday. In March 2001, I received a devastating e-mail explaining that my fortune had disappeared. My wealth evaporated in a fraud [scam] that left me without resources.

"In that instant God confronted me with a choice: die [to self] now or waste away. After forty years, I finally submitted to him. I put my life on the altar and said, 'Lord, I'm yours. Do what you wish. I would rather die than live another day of waste.'

"Today the toys of the desert prison are gone. There are times when I miss the Ferrari and the parties and the trips.

But I would never take my old life back. I was a man who had everything but purpose. God had to take everything away to give me his purpose.

"In the years since God met me in the wilderness, I have been discovering a new world. My wanderings are being used to reach others who are out in the desert. I know their pain. I have discovered that when I have nothing, God is free to make anything he wishes of me.

"This paradigm shift was illustrated in a recent decision about money. My wife went to work for a real estate firm whose ethics were questionable. The stress level was intense.

"After three months, we realized we were making our decisions about work based on our *financial need* rather than on God's priorities. We decided the integrity of our marriage and the values we held were more important than the income. In spite of the fact that we had no other financial provision, my wife quit work. We agreed that honoring God was more important than that income.

"Within a week of making this decision, I received my first paid contract for writing and my wife was asked to work on two consulting design jobs. God provided more income to us than we would have made with the real estate job. But it happened only after we adopted his priorities without knowing how it would unfold. We had to act in trust, without any evidence of provision except his Word.

"This seems to be the pathway of my life. It is a daily adventure—I quite literally never know what the day will bring. But, of course, I never really *did* know. I was deluded by the myth of my own control.

"Now I see that since God is fully in control, I can face each day with rejoicing. 'What will you do with me today, Father?'

is the most exciting life I could live. Fear of the unknown is gone. It has been replaced with trust in the Lord of my life.

"He is God Almighty. Anything can happen."

Author's note: Skip has written a book with Ken Blanchard and Phil Hodges called Words to Lead By: A Practical Daily Devotional on Leading Like Jesus. *I encourage you to read this guide to Jesus's leadership in the marketplace. Skip can be reached at skipmoen@comcast.net.*

POINTS TO PONDER

1. Where do you personally land on the faith/planning paradox?
2. Have you created a family budget?
3. How important is money to you right now?

5
||||||||||||

Skills, Strengths, and Weaknesses That Matter in Ministry

Most of the business skills I learned have been practical in ministry. The application is different, but the principles are the same.

—SURVEY RESPONDENT

Would you expect a healthy, vibrant church to suffer from lax administration or incompetent leadership? I suppose it's possible, but if a church lacks excellence behind the scenes or at the top, it's likely the body of believers it serves will stop finding their church very attractive. An exodus might not be too far behind.

God wants our best—especially in his church. First Corinthians 15:58 says, "Always [excel] in the Lord's work, knowing that your labor in the Lord is not in vain." And Colossians 3:23 admonishes us that no matter what work we do, we should "do it enthusiastically, as something done for the Lord and not for men."

Mediocrity is the primary way to repulse customers in your business or guests in your church. Unpaid bills or an unorganized office may harm a church's reputation in the community and embarrass its members. Low-quality equipment or furniture may distract during worship, as will an off-key choir or a typo-ridden bulletin. Excellence is our calling. When we fall short, we dishonor the Lord himself. Jesus taught us to literally go the extra mile in our service to others: "If anyone forces you to go one mile, go with him two" (Matt. 5:41).

Of course, the workplace is all about excellence and performance too. We want to hire the best people to execute the vision of the organization. If someone consistently underperforms, the company as a whole is affected (and that person is probably not in line with his or her calling anyway).

I'd wager that the times you displayed your most memorable excellence before your boss and the Lord were when your passion, skills, and the task at hand were in perfect alignment. Can you remember an instance when you saw a puzzle-piece fit between your talents and your assignment? I have several such memories in my current job. Even when I sold radio advertising, I can remember flying high after closing a deal and dreaming about my future long-term success.

This chapter is about understanding and refining the marketplace skills you already possess that make you an effective leader in ministry, covering:

- a list of workplace skills that you'll find extremely valuable when applied to full-time ministry
- stories of how others have applied their marketplace skills to their new ministry careers
- an interview with the dean of a distance-learning

church leadership institute that specializes in training
leaders leaving the marketplace

Plus we'll look at another research project that reveals the
strengths and weaknesses of leaders at effective churches.

THE ENTREPRENEURIAL PASTOR

In his book *Pastorpreneur* (Vision Quest, 2003), Dr. John
Jackson coined a new term that resonated with me. He writes,
"A pastorpreneur is an innovative pastor, lay leader, or Christian businessperson—a creative dreamer who is willing to
take great risks with the hope of great gain for Christ and his
kingdom" (excerpted from www.pastorpreneur.com).

Are you entrepreneurial? Do you dream, risk, and strive
to make gains for the Kingdom? We found that former businesspeople who became pastors were significantly more likely
than nonbusiness pastors to engage in the following "risky"
church activities:

- launching a fund-raising campaign
- building a new building or addition
- planting a new church

They were only slightly more likely than their nonbusiness
counterparts to start a new ministry within their church (maybe
because the risk was lower and therefore less attractive to these
pioneers). However, churches with business crossover leaders
were *less* likely to hire a consultant or staff or to send out missionaries. I don't know whether these leaders shied away from
hiring because they had a plethora of volunteers or whether
they retained the business habit of tight cost control—or if
a measure of prideful "I can do it all myself" reared its head.
Either way, their paid staff remained sparse.

The fact that business-to-church leaders send out fewer missionaries concerns me. Is there a theological reason for this, or a simple desire born in the workplace to keep the flock intact and focused on a common, local vision? I can relate to not wanting to lose staff, to keep my best people on my most important projects. But this mind-set is unhealthy in a church environment, stemming from disobedience to the Lord's Great Commission to spread the gospel (see Matt. 28:19–20).

SKILLS, STRENGTHS, AND WEAKNESSES OF CROSSOVER LEADERS

Let's delve deeper into the characteristics of these leaders. We asked subjects, What areas of your leadership and personal growth would you like most to improve? The responses enhanced our understanding of their skills, strengths, and weaknesses.

WEAKNESSES

Top desired areas of personal and professional growth reported by crossover leaders:

- evangelism
- fellowship
- ministry
- budgeting and fund-raising

How do *you* rate in these areas? The surprise was that people from the marketplace feel less than fully adept at church budgeting and fund-raising. Why would church leaders with business backgrounds feel more ill prepared in money matters than their nonbusiness peers? Could it be because they're used to battling budgets and competing for dollars through human strength, whereas leaders with mainly theological training have healthier faith that God will provide?

What's not so surprising about the chart above is that the top three weaknesses are people oriented, whereas the strengths listed below tend to be more strategic or process oriented. I know many extremely capable business executives who wouldn't rate themselves high on evangelizing, ministering to people one-on-one, or building nonbusiness relationships. In fact, some CEOs I know have few personal friends, which they blame on a lack of time.

STRENGTHS

Top personal and professional strengths reported by crossover leaders:
- church administration   • conflict resolution   • prayer

We asked our respondents which skills carried with them into their new role were most beneficial. Their top picks included the following:
- financial planning
- administration and accounting
- vision and strategy
- team leadership
- speaking and writing
- problem solving and decision making
- people skills and conflict management
- overall leadership skills
- time management, organization, and multitasking
- technological ability
- thick skin

Many of these strengths have obvious applications in ministry. Peruse the list again and record your top three skills:

1. _____

2. _____

3. _____

Let these abilities emerge in your new ministry role. Better yet, find a position in which your strongest skills are necessary for getting the job done. Our respondents relayed many personal experiences in which their skills and passions remained intact when they changed careers. When you're good at your work, you'll enjoy it more. And when you enjoy it, it will seem less like work.

The following stories are taken directly from our research results. They reveal fascinating snippets of real-life journeys that will inspire you to examine how your own background, training, or passion could roll right into a ministry position. Notice the broad array of careers that preceded jumps to ministry:

- A former *claims adjuster* is able to "separate the personal from the professional," allowing him to hold back the excess emotional drain when helping his church members get through funerals or other life difficulties.
- A former *video producer* finds that his experience in storytelling helps him teach the Bible.
- A successful *entrepreneur* who developed his people to become his most valuable resource has found that same skill to be invaluable in the church-volunteer setting.
- A former *reporter* who dug for facts now conducts extensive research for his teaching.
- A former *advertising executive* instinctively communicates from the point of view of the people she's trying to reach.

- A former *parole and probation officer* who was trained as a counselor uses those same counseling skills now, only from a biblical perspective.
- A former *salesperson* is more persuasive when he tries to lead people through change.
- A former *attorney* who represented many hurting people is compassionate with people's needs in the church.

God placed you in the workplace for a reason. These teachers, salespeople, claims adjusters, reporters, and hundreds of other professionals found a direct application of their work experience in their ministry career. And you can too.

"I believe the primary reason I followed my earlier path of employment is that God was preparing me to work with the local church to achieve his plans." —Survey respondent

Our research revealed that of all executive pastors, 53 percent came from the business world, whereas 44 percent of senior pastors have a business background. Twenty-seven percent of our survey respondents still work part- or full-time while they engage in ministry.

Many of these leaders were surprised at the intense administrative work required in the church and other ministries. They also overwhelmingly reported that people skills learned on the job toughened their skin, sensitized them to the deeply personal style of ministry work, and seasoned their communication with compassion. So take stock of your own skills and watch for opportunities to use them to glorify God through your new work.

We now turn to the story of my good friend Thom Rainer, whose life experience illustrates the power of a providential call. He has been obedient to various calls throughout his life, including the most recent one as president and CEO of Life-Way Christian Resources.

LIFESTORY

**Dr. Thom Rainer—
From Banker to Pastor to Seminary Dean, Author, and Back to CEO**
Age at first crossover: 25
Former position: VP of corporate lending
Company: SouthTrust
Key quote: "I would encourage every single person in ministry to have some type of business training."

At age twelve Thom Rainer worked as a teller in his father's bank. At thirteen he moved to the consumer loan department. When he graduated near the top of his class, with a major in finance and a minor in statistics, he was already a banking veteran with a decade of experience.

His father, president of the small-town bank, was himself the son of a banker. "Not only did I see my destiny in the banking world," says Thom, "in some ways I felt obligated, because there was a tradition I wanted to continue."

When he turned twenty-five, Thom had already leaped up the corporate ladder as vice president of corporate lending at SouthTrust. His career headed down a path of success and fulfillment. Life in the finance lane was moving fast.

But then God moved in a different direction. Thom got

involved in a church and found a keen interest in his Sunday school class. He eventually became a deacon and a new goal sprouted in his ambitious heart: become one of the best in high finance and extend his Christian witness throughout the national marketplace. Banking and the Bible propelled his personal vision.

"But something started happening within my spirit," Thom says. "I was beginning to get an uneasiness about my career, which was really strange because I always loved banking, had always loved working with corporations. And yet I found myself not getting the same fulfillment. I wanted to do things with the church all the time."

While Thom rationalized that any Christian business person needed to be involved in church, he still found more joy in the church than in the financial world. Eventually he didn't want to do banking or business any longer.

For a few months he tried to deny this call toward vocational ministry. He led Bible studies at the bank, vainly hoping God would reciprocate by restoring his joy in banking. "I wanted him to take away this absurd idea that I was to be a pastor or preacher or some other weird creature."

Shift number three jolted him once and for all. In 1982 some friends in the church asked him to pray for their five-year-old son, Brian, who needed open-heart surgery. He rejoiced with the parents when Brian's operation was successful. A couple of days later Thom decided to visit the boy while he recovered.

"When I got into the car, I had this keen awareness that Brian was going to die. I did not want to accept that, but now I know it was God speaking. I rushed to pediatric intensive care, and the moment I walked into his cubicle, he flatlined. The medical personnel pushed me and his parents out of the way and tried to revive him, but it was to no avail. Brian was dead at five years old."

The boy's parents held onto Thom's shoulders. In the midst of panic, sobs, and bustling nurses, he sensed God speaking to him: "Thom, as you are caring for these my sheep, you will be a shepherd to many."

That traumatic moment was the culmination of God's pull on his life. Though Brian was in heaven, Thom knew his calling was to the sheep still on earth. He drove home and grieved in his wife's arms. When his intense anguish and shock subsided, he told his wife, Nellie Jo, "Sit down. I have something else to tell you."

She smiled and said, "God's called you into ministry, hasn't he?"

Thom submitted his resignation three days later. Within thirty days he left the bank, sold his house, enrolled in a seminary he knew little about and moved to Louisville, Kentucky. He attended Southern Baptist Theological Seminary from 1983 to 1988 and received his PhD.

"If God calls you, don't go with fear and trepidation about how this is all going to be done. Step unto the sea of faith and walk on that water and just watch the miracles take place."   — Thom Rainer

---

His ensuing opportunities included four pastorates, a career as dean of the Billy Graham School at Southern Seminary, numerous speaking engagements around the world, research projects, and myriad book projects on church health and leadership. He now serves as president and CEO of LifeWay, a four-thousand-employee organization and a pillar of the Southern Baptist Convention.

"Do I have any regrets?" Thom asks. "The answer is very

simple, very loud, very profound. No! To be in the will of God is the greatest joy of life."

Thom offers four pieces of advice to those investigating their own call to ministry:

1. *When God calls, immediately obey.* "You will never have any joy and you will have a restlessness that cannot be stilled until you obey. If a business person is sensing God's calling, respond to that call. Do not delay."

2. *Get training.* "For some, it would be the path of seminary; for others, it would be some other type of training. But just as one is not prepared to go into a business role without training, one is not prepared to go into the ministry without some type of significant training. And whatever path you decide to take, whatever route you decide to go as you cross over from the world of business to the world of vocational ministry, I would definitely advise that you train."

3. *Be financially prepared.* "Many people who've gone from the business world to ministry are not aware that ministry is not the highest paying job in the world. Ministry, especially during the time of training, can be a struggle. One common reason that students drop out of seminary is that they were not financially prepared for the transition into the ministry world."

4. *Make certain your spouse is a part of the call.* "If they are not, your life will be miserable. I have never had to suffer that reality, but I have many acquaintances and friends who have, and for the most part, they have stayed in misery during their venture into vocational ministry, or in some cases, their marriages have failed. If the spouse is not in this, I do not advise going forward into ministry."

BENEFITS OF BUSINESS EXPERIENCE

Thom derived so much benefit from his time in the marketplace that he advises all seminary students to secure some type of business training to learn budgeting/administration skills and basic people skills.

He likens churches to companies with sizable budgets. Even small churches may deal with a quarter of a million dollars; large congregations can run tens of millions through their books every year. Unfortunately, many leaders don't know how to read a financial statement, understand the implications of debt repayment, or grasp basic cash management principles. These shortcomings, Thom says, can easily be alleviated by business training.

All three of his sons were finance majors. Two of them felt called into vocational ministry. Thom urged them to spend time in the business world first to fully understand the administrative side of the church.

He also sees the wisdom of joining the business world to hone people skills. "Many students who go straight from college to seminary to their first church without any 'real world' experience do not know how to relate to people in their church." These "innocent doves" have bypassed the encounters the business world offers—both the good and the bad—which can all be used for God's glory.

ADDITIONAL RESEARCH ON LEADERSHIP STRENGTHS AND WEAKNESSES

Thom has written volumes on church health, leadership, and church consulting and growth. His research has yielded much more than he could fit in his many books, and he has graciously allowed me to summarize a small part of that work in this book.

According to Thom, an effective church attracts the unchurched and grows as a result of its outreach. Implied in this definition of effectiveness is how well the church fulfills its biblical purposes (see Acts 2:42–47). A study he and his team conducted a few years ago focused on the strengths and weaknesses of leaders of effective churches, rather than on a specific group of pastors who left the marketplace. The leaders' best practices—as well as their admitted deficiencies—are worth noting as you examine your own gifts and shortcomings. Let's touch on a few of their top weaknesses first.

Top Weaknesses of Effective Church Pastors

Pastoral ministry. Leaders of effective churches fall short in this category, but that's not necessarily a negative. The Rainer research team was surprised to discover that leaders of effective churches spent ten hours per week in pastoral care, while leaders of the comparison churches spent twenty-three hours in the same type of ministries.

One pastor from Nevada tells the Rainer research team, "If I get a consistent criticism, it is my failure to live up to the expectations to minister to each person individually. But if I lived up to all their expectations, I wouldn't have time for sermon preparation, personal evangelism, and just plain ol' dreaming. I constantly live with this tension but refuse to give up time from the responsibilities."

But if this "flaw" exists in the most effective churches, then the conclusion is that you as the pastor don't have to excel in ministry tasks like counseling, hospital visits, weddings and funerals to lead a church of excellence.

Base your role on advice from the book of Acts: when the leader ministers by the Word and prayer, others in the church are unleashed and empowered to contribute to the care of those being ministered to:

> In those days, as the number of the disciples was multiplying, there arose a complaint by the Hellenistic Jews against the Hebraic Jews that their widows were being overlooked in the daily distribution. Then the Twelve summoned the whole company of the disciples and said, "It would not be right for us to give up preaching about God to wait on tables. Therefore, brothers, select from among you seven men of good reputation, full of the Spirit and wisdom, whom we can appoint to this duty. But we will *devote ourselves to prayer and to the preaching ministry.*" (Acts 6:1–4, emphasis mine)

Task driven and impatient. While getting things done is a positive attribute of effective leaders, the leaders themselves rank it as a defect in their personal style that kept them from developing rich connections with the people around them. We do revere executives and pastors who drive forward to achieve goals and visions, but productivity can be a leadership limitation when it gets out of balance. Many top pastors say this trait manifests itself at the expense of fellowship and to the exclusion of relational issues, including building relationships with church members and staff. A pastor from North Carolina says, "I get so focused on a project that I often fail to take people's feelings into consideration. It's good to be task driven, but it's not good to be so driven that you forget about people." Another pastor says, "When I move so fast that the people don't know what's going on, I run into obstacles, criticisms, and apathy. I'm trying to learn that you just can't communicate too much."

Related weaknesses reported by ministers were "lack of patience" and "dealing with staff"—casualties of a task-driven style.

Consider some quotes from the research:

"No area of ministry frustrates me more than dealing with staff. I feel so inept."

"My worst mistakes in ministry have mostly been related to issues with the ministry team."

"The two greatest conflicts I have had in ministry had to do with firing a staff member and not dealing with a weak staff member."

Let's briefly look at a few more shortcomings reported by the effective church pastors.

Dealing with criticism. Almost seven out of ten leaders note this as a weakness. An Evangelical Free Church pastor says, "Reaching the unchurched is spiritual warfare. Attacks and criticisms are to be expected, but we cannot give up on the Great Commission just because our feelings have been hurt."

An effective way to diffuse criticism is to prevent it. The research team found that the leaders admitted their weaknesses without hesitation. This paradox is reminiscent of the "Level 5 Leader" in Jim Collins' *Good to Great:* when you admit your weaknesses, you actually strengthen your leadership.

One of Thom's researchers talked to a thirty-two-year-old mother of two who had become a Christian only five months earlier. She said the main reason she chose her current church was the pastor. "More than anything else was

Bruce's transparency," she said, "his willingness to admit mistakes. He is just a real person."

"Real people" make mistakes. If your critics see you stumble at times like they themselves do, they might be more forgiving or patient. Admit your faults, identify your failures—and you'll often steal your church members' critical thunder.

Bad time management. These pastors worry about their lack of family time, Bible study, and prayer. But their greatest lament is needing to spend more time in personal evangelism. (Evangelism, by the way, was the top shortcoming reported by leaders who came from the marketplace.) Even though the pastors spend on average five hours a week in personal evangelism, they typically feel this isn't enough. One point to note is that these effective leaders are more self-critical than others. Sharing the gospel for five hours a week may be satisfactory for the comparison church leaders.

Failure to develop a strategic plan. Slightly more than half the pastors say they don't plan well for the long-term or fail altogether to develop a strategic plan for their church. One of the reasons the leaders express concern over this perceived weakness is related to their passionate desire to reach the unchurched. "I need something to keep me on focus to reach people for Christ," says a pastor from Illinois. "If I could just get a plan in place, I think I would have a more intense and intentional focus to reach the unchurched."

TOP STRENGTHS OF LEADERS OF EFFECTIVE CHURCHES

The top strengths mentioned by the leaders in the Rainer research project relate to reaching the unchurched. The churches these people lead are among the most effective in the country at spreading the gospel and discipling new members. Here are their key strengths.

Vision. Bob Russell, the recently retired senior minister of my church, Southeast Christian Church in Louisville, Kentucky, says he didn't begin with a vision forty years ago. Rather, over time a vision found the church (now one of the largest in North America). He never planned to be the pastor of such a large church. Instead, he says, "We just tried to be obedient to what God called us to do and do everything with excellence."

Another pastor from Ohio tells a similar story. "When I came to the church nine years ago, the church did not have a clue where it was going. The leaders told me that they were willing to follow me anywhere if I could just tell them where we needed to go."

The ability to cast vision does not always mean that the leader knows precisely where the church should go. He may communicate that obedience to the Great Commission is imperative, that reaching the unchurched is not an option, and that ministering to those in need is the cultural mandate for the church. But the leader of the church may not have a clear idea where this obedience to God may lead.

Two elements of vision casting are prevalent with these pastors. First, the leader is confident because of his experience and faith that God will ultimately direct the church's vision. Second, he communicates the vision with passion and inspiration.

A female attendee in one of the effective churches says, "When Pastor Paul talks about the vision for our church, the whole church gets fired up. We believe in God's vision for our church because the pastor is so enthusiastic about it."

Rarely do these leaders say they developed precise plans to lead their churches to growth. But one point is clear: regardless of the lack of detail, *the communicated vision in almost all of the Rainer team's surveys includes a clear and compelling picture of reaching lost people.* A pastor's urgency to reach the unchurched is a vision in itself.

Humor. The formerly unchurched indicate they are attracted to a particular church because of the personality and transparency of the pastor. And often they mention that the personality included a sense of humor.

The surprise, however, is the number of leaders who mention humor as a strength. Nearly seven out of ten leaders note this strength, the second most frequently mentioned characteristic of leadership.

"Many of the unchurched expect a real straightlaced pastor when they finally visit a church," a Nazarene pastor says. "They are really surprised to find we are human just like they are. A sense of humor tends to disarm those who may be uptight about being in church."

Persistence. The pastor of a nondenominational church in Maryland says his leadership strengths could be summed up in one word: persistence.

"I have been at this church for fourteen years. I've made some stupid mistakes, and I've done a few good things. As I look back over fourteen years, I can see that God has blessed me despite me. Too many of my fellow pastors run to another church at the first sign of trouble. I'm glad I stuck it out."

The persistence issue is more than just hanging on for several years. These leaders are tenacious in their attempts to get God's work done well at the churches they serve.

Leadership by example. A Presbyterian pastor from Virginia says, "One of my greatest leadership strengths is my willingness to lead by example. I have a lot of weaknesses, but that is my greatest strength."

A majority of the pastors say that to be effective, they had to model personal evangelism more than any other trait. Here are some of their comments:

"The senior pastor must model personal evange-lism to the staff and congregation."

"The pastor should set the example by seeking to lead one person to the Lord each week."

"I must set the pace in personal evangelism. I can't expect the people to do what the pastor is not doing."

"The pastor must be a soul winner. Personal evan-gelism is both taught and caught."

"I must establish relationships with non-Christians so that the people in the church will see my lifestyle modeled."

"The pastor is a player/coach. He shows evange-lism by example then encourages and exhorts others to do evangelism."

The issue of leadership by example is most conspicuous in the comments on personal evangelism, but it is not limited to that one issue. Other pastors say they try to model what they believe their staff and members should do in prayer, per-sonal Bible study, ethical issues, and family issues, to name a few. Pastors must be biblical examples, practicing what they preach.

Faith and optimism. "What impressed me about the pas-tor of Valley Community Church," says a church attender, "was his confidence in God. He made me almost believe that anything was possible through God—and I wasn't even a believer at the time!"

Slightly more than half of the pastors indicate their faith in God was a leadership strength.

"I have taken what many people would call stupid risks. We recently entered into a building program that is a huge step of faith," a Texas pastor says. "We will have to grow our budget by 25 percent within two years to be able to carry out this project. But I am convinced that God will provide. And the people of the church have followed my leadership. They are convinced too."

Some of the leaders are careful describing this particular strength.

One New Jersey pastor says, "I know that my faith and optimism are strengths God has given me. But I don't want you to tell people . . . that my theology is the power of positive thinking or name-it-and-claim-it."

Faith and optimism are contagious. More than one leader says they challenge their churches to do something so great that it is doomed to failure unless God is in it.

Relational skills. Thom writes, "In the year 2000 I made a decision as dean of the Southern Baptist Theological Seminary that our faculty would add a required course in leadership to cover such topics as conflict management, financial management, and interpersonal skills. The [third] topic in particular was one that I knew to be of urgent import. I have seen, both as a dean and as a church consultant, some of the brightest people blow opportunities for effective leadership because they have poor interpersonal skills."

A majority of the leaders in his study cite interpersonal skills as one of their strengths. An executive pastor from Ohio says, "I've got five good friends who graduated with me from seminary. Two have lost their jobs and are not in ministry. Another is in a difficult situation in a church. I believe the common factor in all of my friends' problems is their failure in relating to people. Their problems are a lesson for me. I'm trying to improve my relational skills even though I think I'm pretty good at it."

While all these personal strengths equip church leaders for the tough work of ministering and preaching, I'd like to leave you with one of the strengths your flock will expect in abundance: theological expertise. Seminary training is available in many flavors—distance learning, traditional classes, residencies, seminars, and independent projects—and I guarantee there's a perfect training institute out there for you.

Let's look in depth at one such option.

THE LONDEN INSTITUTE: MINISTRY TRAINING FOR SUCCESSFUL PROFESSIONALS

I had the opportunity to interview Dr. Bob Pavelsky, dean of the Londen Institute of Evangelism, Graduate School of Ministry in Corona, California. The school's mission is to provide ministry training for people who have already had successful careers and now feel called to go into church leadership. It also trains church leaders to step up to the next level in their ministry.

AUTHOR: What trends have you seen in the last few years regarding people moving from the workplace to vocational ministry?

PAVELSKY: Since my days as a student, I have observed a growing trend of people leaving the marketplace for ministry. In the 1960s and '70s they tended to be fifty-plus and were very frustrated with their work. Ministry gave them an opportunity to work in a more constructive, positive environment. Through the '80s, '90s, and now 2000s, the age seems to be going down. More people in their mid- to late-thirties are leaving the marketplace to go into ministry. These people seem not to be frustrated or unhappy in their work but feel a strong call of God on their lives, leading them into ministry. At the Londen Institute Graduate School of Ministry we recently enrolled a retired couple in our program. I think we are going to see more of this as retirees stop thinking of retirement as spending the last phase of their lives in leisure and begin to think of that phase as retiring from having to earn a paycheck, so they can occupy themselves with endeavors of significance for themselves and others.

Author: Are there any other demographic or psychographic similarities among the people you see making this transition?

Pavelsky: The major similarity I see is that these second-career people want practical training. They tend to be more interested in learning *how* to do it rather than the academic ramifications of it. Years ago, someone wanting a second career in ministry typically had to return to school full time and pursue a traditional academic course of study. I believe those of us in ministerial training learned some very important lessons from ITT, DeVry, and others: people want just enough academics to learn how to do it. [So] we have developed practical, professional training for second-career people called to ministry. This kind of training is appropriate for successful second-career people since they have, either in previous schooling or through their life's work, developed the basic skills that young people obtain in the first two to three years of college. A practical, professional model is definitely not the recommended choice for the recent high school graduate. Eighteen- to twenty-two-year-olds need to attend a traditional college to get the basics and to mature a few years. The college freshman may believe he or she is totally committed to a field, only to find that by their junior year they have changed their mind three to seven times, depending on whose statistics you are reading.

AUTHOR: What is the typical course selection and/or degree program these crossover leaders choose?

PAVELSKY: At the Londen Institute Graduate School of Ministry we focus on practical, professional training. We don't ignore academic foundations. We require our students both at the bachelor's and master's levels to take coursework in six different areas: biblical interpretation, church history, Bible survey, communication and preaching, apologetics, and theology. All of the courses are designed to be applicable to real-life settings and are as practical as we can make them while giving students a sound biblical foundation. The courses are taught by way of distance learning.

Our students also attend four residencies of ten to twelve days each over a two-year period. The residencies follow a "learn ministry from those that do ministry" model. We bring in church leaders at the top of the profession to teach entrepreneurial leadership, pastoral care, church administration, church planting and revitalization, communication (preaching and advertising), inner-city ministry, and church programming.

AUTHOR: What advice would you have for someone considering crossing over into ministry?

PAVELSKY: Pray and obey. I don't believe this is something that should be done only because [people] are tired or frustrated with their jobs. Regardless of how they feel about their jobs, crossing over into ministry should be done as a response to God's call. When someone gets that call, do what it says and look for ways to get the necessary training from a school that will meet their needs. Because these students are adults who have already demonstrated their abilities in the workforce, I believe the best school for them follows the practical, professional model rather than the traditional model.

Certainly training of any kind will benefit the crossover ministry leader. Thom's winding road that led him from business to ministry to academia and back to nonprofit business is atypical, though he is not alone. Others have journeyed between the workplace and ministry in both directions. Still others remain in business but consider themselves "marketplace ministers," a new type of ministry leader aptly described in *God@Work* by Rich Marshall and Ken Walker (Destiny Image Publishers, 2005).

"I loved and appreciated every minute of my seminary education—it was one of the most rewarding seasons of my life, but I think we have got to start training people on some of the rudimentary skills of administration and leadership."   —Survey respondent

---

When you combine training with well-honed skills, personal passions, and spiritual gifts, your potential in God's new calling can be staggering. For the Lord will work through you in your area of giftedness and will fuel your passions according to his purposes. His plans will unfold in front of you, and you'll wonder why it took so long to find this sweet spot in your life.

No one else can fulfill the specific purpose for which God has equipped you. Take your skills seriously. Hone them. Grow them.

Then watch the Lord build them into a masterpiece.

POINTS TO PONDER

1. Do you agree that excellence is important in all areas of a church?
2. What are your personal strengths and weaknesses that relate to ministry?

6
||||||||||||

Dealing with Challenges in Ministry

I thought church people were different! . . .
I've found working on staff in churches can be
like entering someone's kingdom.
—SURVEY RESPONDENTS

M y goal throughout this book is to encourage you to seek God's plan for your desire to enter the ministry. And though the grass on the other side of the fence may look greener right now, some brown patches await you. This chapter will help prepare you for a couple of them.

PART 1: LONELINESS AND FEAR

If you've been a manager, CEO, supervisor, or any other kind of leader in the marketplace, you understand that life at the top offers rich blessings and stark disappointments. It can be lonely as often as it is exciting. And sometimes inspiration gives way to doses of fear.

I have deep respect for pastors in the lonely spotlight, where the attacks of the enemy can be as relentless as they are furious—and where arrows shot from within your own ranks can pierce you.

Let's tackle loneliness and fear before they have a chance to sneak up on you. Prevention can be the best defense. While you will surely cross paths with these leadership maladies, the main idea of this section is that you are truly not alone and have nothing to fear.

Guaranteed.

Now You're "Them"

As a pew-sitter, you observed, participated, worshipped, and learned. You probably felt little pressure to perform. Your minister and other leaders carried the ball during the service. Maybe you taught Sunday school, served as a deacon, or administered Communion, but your senior pastor bore the bulk of the leadership responsibility.

When you become a vocational church leader, you cross the "us vs. them" gap—a very real journey. No longer can you listen to complaints about your church while you observe from the sidelines. Now you are a target for criticism and blame whenever an outspoken member steps up to the scrimmage line.

Suddenly you're in the fish bowl. People watch every word, deed, and action to see if you're living up to their image of a church leader. Your family is in the fish bowl with you— privacy is minimized, everyone stares, and you can't escape the glass. Sometimes you'll feel overrun by critics, but displaying humility or retreating from the fight will only draw complaints about your "weak leadership." You are a new creation in the eyes of the congregation. You're no longer in the audience—your pew seat has moved to the stage.

I'm exaggerating the life of the new church leader to help prepare you for a new, strange land where your flock will surprise and disappoint you. People are still people even when they sit in a pew. Sadly, our sin nature seeps into our church lives, and as we'll see in a moment, can grow in unexpected directions. Church is one of the few institutions where people who pay so little demand so much.

"The emotional and spiritual drain is tremendous. I worked more hours in the corporate world than I do now, but the drain is twice as much."

—Survey respondent

Needy (and sometimes whiny) members produce stress, exhaustion, depression, and emotional distance. The result is bruised or nonexistent relationships. No longer can you just smile at fellow attenders from across the aisle or chat for a few minutes over coffee. Their lives are entrusted into your hands. Their problems are deposited into your account.

"Loneliness is zapping," says a business-to-ministry leader. "I've lost the ability to share personal frustrations with anyone at church."

An unexpected finding in our research was the unintended solitude of so many pastors. How can people who minister to so many, who speak to a crowd every week, languish in loneliness? Don't pastors work with people all day long and preach to them in droves? You can't get to the preacher through the throng after a service. They're always in demand. Their calendars bulge with commitments.

Nevertheless, the lonely pastor is common in today's churches. You will likely toy with loneliness during your ministry career, especially if you become a senior minister. You may fight the following circumstances, if only temporarily:

- Your close relationships are damaged by the spotlight on your life.
- You lose daily contact with a close group of peers.
- Your list of friends grows short.
- You get little recognition for hard work.

If your staff is small or only part-time, you could wind up a one-man show on a typical day. Phone messages, e-mails, sermon preparation, bill paying, hospital visits, community events, and countless responsibilities can cut you off from close human contact and leave little room for relationships.

But even if you're fortunate to work closely with a few people in an office, they may be your subordinates or volunteers. Your interpersonal contact with them could be limited to church business and ministry work. You may get to know them well, but intimate friendships rarely find footholds without deeper roots.

Lest you think I'm down on ministry gigs, let me assure you that I'm merely passing on the comments of leaders who crossed over from the marketplace. Plus, I believe it honors God to caution people about what they might experience in a chosen life direction. Otherwise, they might get broadsided, as I did in my first job.

When I graduated college, I craved a career in radio with starry-eyed innocence. I loved music. DJs were gods to me. I dreamed of producing jingles and starring in commercials. I admired the morning show radio hosts—all I needed was to get on the air and my personal problems would disappear too.

I couldn't cut it behind a microphone, so I settled for selling ad spots. Just hanging around the music, studio, and fans thrilled me. I applied for an account executive job and got an interview.

The sales manager, Steve Fehder, must've seen something in this hungry, still-living-with-mom, green college grad. But I'll never forget his sudden change in tone in my second interview. Steve said something like, "You're going to start at the bottom in this job. I'm going to throw the Yellow Pages at you, and you'll have to build your own account list from it. Cold-calling will be your life. You're going to knock on new doors every day. The first two to three years will be extremely tough. If you survive, you'll do great, but most don't make it that far."

He paused. I blinked in disbelief. Could it be that bad? Why did he dash my enthusiasm with such cruelty?

But he couldn't sour me on my dream job. My vision was clear, my path paved all the way to the horizon. I would achieve greatness.

"Oh, I can do it. No problem."

His eyes leveled with mine. "What makes you think you'll be any different?"

We talked for awhile longer. I must've convinced him with my naive sincerity, because he offered me the job. Later he admitted it was all a test—he wanted to see if selling me *off* my dream by describing the worst-case scenario would actually increase my resolve to succeed. He wondered if I would rise to the challenge.

That important lesson shaped who I am. And I'd like to offer the same honest forecast for you.

Church members, the people who will be your collective boss, fight their own evil natures just like the rest of humanity. "All have sinned and fall short of the glory of God" (Rom. 3:23). We didn't sin a long time ago and wake up perfect one Sunday morn; we still sin and sin and sin in many different ways. It's why I don't keep a daily journal—I don't want my kids to know how often I succumb to sin and fail to exhibit the fruit of the Spirit.

When you cross over, people will still be people. In fact, as a guru once said, "Wherever you go, there you are." Don't expect fireworks and confetti to greet you just because you feel called. Yes, there may be excitement, warmth, even gifts when you commit to ministry. But every job—even as a morning-show DJ—soon becomes just a job. Your passion and the Lord himself will ensure your calling in the midst of other fallen humans who will often bring you down with them. If and when your passion wanes, you will have to rest in the faith of your God-given personal ministry vision.

Ironically, it's those times when loneliness may creep into your heart. Let's look at how to fight back.

THREE WEAPONS TO BATTLE LEADERSHIP LONELINESS

Be encouraged—you aren't empty-handed in the struggle against solitude. If your gray days seem to drag on in your ministry position, review the following three keys to loneliness prevention. If you develop these habits, you can enjoy more balanced relationships that keep the blues at bay.

1. Develop an inner circle of staff or lay leaders. Jesus built an intimate band of followers, namely Peter, James, and John. These disciples accompanied the Lord on special occasions. He singled them out for special conversations and teaching. They are always listed among the first few names whenever the twelve are mentioned in Scripture.

Jesus didn't spend equal time and attention with all the disciples. His example is a wise leadership lesson: invest most of your limited time in only a few people—preferably the ones with the most leadership potential—rather than on your entire staff. The outcome is closer and more manageable relationships, fewer demands on your time, and greater ministry results. You can't intimately befriend a group—Jesus himself didn't.

When you impart wisdom, training, and love to a few quality people, they return loyalty, productivity, and love in kind. But the returns don't stop with you—the benefits extend to those your inner circle leads, teaches, or shepherds. This is human multiplication at its finest. They propel your church in new directions, through different doors that produce harvests you never dreamed of achieving. Your effectiveness broadens and deepens when you invest yourself into a handful of gifted followers or coleaders.

2. Keep your work in perspective. Now that your church and work lives have merged (or are about to), the boundaries you once drew between the office, home, and church may blur and flex. The phone rings at all hours of the night with people's problems and needs. You can't take the weekends off any more, and the one day you choose for your Sabbath buckles under the pelting of nonstop ministry demands. "If *we* have to work," your church members reason, "then why isn't my pastor on the job too?" Unless you spread the responsibilities of your ministry, you're like an on-call doctor that never sleeps.

You've no doubt fought overload throughout your career. The difference in the church world is the "good works" of ministry can burn out the edges of your life if you don't limit their flame.

Let's return to the wise words of Solomon in Ecclesiastes 3:1: "There is an occasion for everything, / and a time for every activity under heaven." When your people start crowding in with cries for help, when the critics raise their voices, when the enemy surrounds you and lays siege to your innermost thoughts, rest in the Lord's encouraging promise: every activity will have its own time. Pursue your Sabbath with the same fervor you give to your responsibilities. Guard and gird your marriage and family time with prayerful determination. Schedule and protect quiet moments with God.

Ask the limitless Lord to find time for every commitment in your finite schedule. He will surprise you with efficiency, effectiveness, and progress. He will guide your steps if you give him control of your daily walk. When I cry out to him in the midst of a crushing workload or stifling stress, he gives me a new day. When my steps are dogged by exhaustion, he delivers me into sweet respite.

Pray for perspective on your work. View your ministry career from eternity and in the light of Scripture. Ask the Lord to show you the most important tasks and conversations he wants you to focus on today.

Just as you walk by faith, *work* by faith. And remember the Lord won't leave you to suffer under the weight alone.

3. Latch on to your current friends. Your friends are important weapons against loneliness. They know you better than your new followers do. They remember you before the ministry spotlight glistened. They understand the inner you, the person behind the ministry mask. If they know you're tired, depressed, frustrated, sad, or bored, your secret is safe with them. No matter how believable your facade on a Sunday morning, you can't hide for long from these trusted souls. You won't be alone for long if you dump your troubles on a tight-lipped friend.

Whether you maintain longtime friendships or spark new ones in the church, don't forget them in your increasing busyness. Always dedicate lunches, coffee, e-mails, or phone time to important relationships. Sometimes I go for months without contacting any close friends, and when we finally get together, it's like a minireunion. When we meet, the old smile is back on my face, my guard is relaxed, frustrations loosen their grip on me as my anxieties flow out in comfortable discussion. I always enjoy refuge in those times. If your friends shy away because of your new "churchy" life, don't contribute to the distance. Reach out. Hold on. You'll need them.

"A lot of Christian friends thought we just might be nuts . . . you know, midlife crisis, etc."   —Survey respondent

Even if your friends raise an eyebrow or two at your new career choice, they should love you anyway. Those who accept you no matter the circumstances deserve your devotion. Give attention to them as the years pass by. They'll give you so much more in return.

FEAR AND THE LEADER

What do you fear most? Our respondents listed the following:

- failure in their new ministry career
- rejection from friends and family
- financial troubles
- inadequate experience or skills
- lost secular contacts
- confusion about where God is leading

As the Great Depression gripped our nation in 1933, President Franklin Delano Roosevelt delivered the sentence that achieved cliché status: "We have nothing to fear but fear itself." His personal resolve to defeat the disastrous economy was the foundation for our turnaround.

As a pastor or ministry leader in the church, we cannot display fear without shock rising from the flock. "Not you," they protest. "You're supposed to be our fearless leader." Can you imagine the outcome if FDR hadn't attacked the Depression like a foreign invader? Our shoulders must not buckle under strain either. We must set our jaws against an uncertain future. And lest we set off a wave of anxiety, we must quell any ripple of concern when those around us fret.

The list of church leadership worries can stretch down the page. How will we pay for the mortgage and cover payroll next month? What do we do about the sudden exodus of members? How can we continue to support a stagnant church plant or new ministry? How do I handle personal verbal attacks on my family from within the church?

You've faced your share of fear in the marketplace for sure. The emotion is real. We can't escape it no matter our vocation.

Many agents can create fear. The Bible touches on three specific sources of trepidation that haunt many ministers.

1. *Our own lack of faith*—when I'm afraid of something, I worry about it. And when I worry, I display faithlessness in God's provision. "Therefore don't worry about tomorrow, because tomorrow will worry about itself. Each day has enough trouble of its own" (Matt. 6:34).

2. *Our enemy*—our adversary is strong and commands respect. He has been known to inflict "thorns in the flesh" on many biblical greats like Paul and Job. Another power Satan is allowed to wield against us

is a mysterious ability to impede our progress: "So we wanted to come to you—even I, Paul, time and again—but Satan hindered us" (1 Thess. 2:18). The devil also deceives with counterfeit miracles, signs, and wonders, and he will cause others to accuse you wrongfully. When we're aware of the enemy's schemes against us, it's all too easy for fear to rear its head. My sinful tendency toward self-reliance contributes to this fear, but I must remember I'm not the one fighting.

3. *Successful competition*—"When Saul observed that David was very successful, he dreaded him" (1 Sam. 18:15). When a competitor achieves greatness, and you haven't moved an inch, how does that make you feel? Humbled? Reluctant to try to keep up? How will you respond?

THE RIGHT KIND OF FEAR

The book of Psalms teaches that fear of the Lord, not man, leads to goodness that men can see. When we realize God's power over us—and fear what he could do if we reject him—we suddenly realize his goodness in our lives. If we tremble at what a person might do to us, how much more should we shudder at the almighty God of the universe's response to our rebellion and sin!

How great is Your goodness
that You have stored up for those who fear You,
and accomplished in the sight of everyone
for those who take refuge in You.
You hide them in the protection of Your presence;
You conceal them in a shelter

from the schemes of men,
from quarrelsome tongues. (Ps. 31:19–20)

When men scheme against us, when we are the butt of false accusations, we are protected. And when we place our fear in the proper place, the schemers and accusers will see the Lord's goodness poured out on us. The book of Psalms is full of this encouragement. Let's take a look at another of my favorites—Psalm 34 by King David.

DAVID—CONFIDENCE IN THE FACE OF FEAR

As kids we learned about David's legendary victory over Goliath. Curiously, after he toppled the Philistine army's fiercest warrior with one shot, he dismembered Goliath's head with the giant's own sword and displayed the bloody trophy for all Jerusalem to see. David also gathered his enemy's weapons into his tent as spoils from battle.

David's career as a military hero was off to a raging start. The Bible says God was with him in all his successful exploits. The entire people of Israel loved him because he delivered consistent victories. King Saul offered his daughters to him in marriage. Soldiers sang boastful songs about this humble, strong leader around campfires. But as his successes mounted, King Saul grew afraid of him.

I highly recommend you read all of Psalm 34 before continuing with this chapter. When David wrote it, he was on the run from a jealous, demon-controlled King Saul and ended up in Gath, a neighboring Philistine country. David's cover was blown in the court of the king of Gath, and he feigned insanity—even drooling down his beard—in front of this king

(1 Sam. 21:13), who sent him away in disgust. What kind of fear could drive this godly, successful, revered leader to debase himself and act like a madman?

I can hear David crying out in that royal court: "Lord, help me! I'm in the hands of the enemy. I've killed thousands of his citizens. I have no idea what to do. Have all my successes led to this final moment? Am I about to die?"

Have you ever felt that desperate? Fear can force us to behave in strange ways. Who knows what I'll do when my back's against the wall? David could not fend off fear even with the confidence he had rightfully earned. It's somehow comforting to know this biblical hero was human too. His valuable lesson is this: no matter how successful you are in work, ministry, and life, fear doesn't care.

Psalm 34 offers four strategies in defending ourselves against fear. David's experience in the hands of the Philistine king can apply to us today, whether we're in the church or marketplace—or in between.

Before the battle, don't forget to suit up with spiritual armor. It also helps to achieve a military mind-set, which means you must understand who your real enemy is and his preferred modus operandi: "Finally, be strengthened by the Lord and by His vast strength. Put on the full armor of God so that you can stand against the tactics of the Devil. For our battle is not against flesh and blood, but against the rulers, against the authorities, against the world powers of this darkness, against the spiritual forces of evil in the heavens" (Eph. 6:10–12).

When your mind is alert to attacks from the spiritual world, your defensive strategy will be more effective. You'll recognize enemy tactics before they bear fruit. Let's see how David exhorts us to fight against the common satanic weapon of fear.

1. He praised the Lord in the midst of his fear. "I will praise the LORD at all times; / His praise will always be on my lips" (Ps. 34:1).

A sign of a healthy spiritual life is praising God no matter the circumstances. Another indicator of maturity is obedience. In this verse, David is obeying the Lord's command to praise him always, even if the enemy threatens to kill him.

2. He gave his fears to God.
I sought the LORD, and He answered me
and delivered me from all my fears. . . .
The righteous cry out, and the LORD hears,
and delivers them from all their troubles. (Ps. 34:4, 17)

Have you ever "cried out"? Have you ever been so desperate, defeated, or depressed that all you could do was crumble before the Lord? If you suffer this intensely, not only will he deliver you at the right time, but he will be close to you: "The LORD is near the brokenhearted; / He saves those crushed in spirit" (v. 18). He will be at your side and comfort you in the midst of your agony.

David knew God could handle every fear on his list. God can release you from yours too.

3. He waited for the Lord to answer his prayers with power. "The angel of the LORD encamps / around those who fear Him, and rescues them" (Ps. 34:7).

According to this verse, when you fear the Lord, you attract a mighty angel who sets up camp around you and exerts the will of the Lord on your behalf.

In my fear and worry, I have struggled to learn the concept of waiting on the Lord over the years. To help, I collected verses that speak directly about *how* to wait on him. These passages have given me great encouragement. The list of summary statements below feeds me when I'm down or desperate for hope:

- Wait in expectation (Ps. 27:14; Ps. 33:20).
- Be strong (Ps. 27:14).
- Take heart (Ps. 27:14).
- Trust him (Prov. 3:5).
- Do not rely on your own understanding (Prov. 3:5).
- Acknowledge him (Prov. 3:6).
- Do not fear (Prov. 3:6).
- Be still (Ps. 37:7).
- Be diligent (Prov. 21:5).
- Lay requests before him (Ps. 5:3).
- Delight in him (Ps. 37:4).
- Commit your plans to the Lord (Prov. 16:3).
- Don't wear yourself out (Prov. 23:4).

These commands, drawn from various verses in the Bible, are a powerful defense against fear and worry. Write them down and stick them on your computer screen. Better yet, memorize a few and call on them silently when fear creeps into your heart. For further encouragement from Scripture on waiting, look up the following verses: Psalm 5:3, 27:14, 33:20, 40:1, and 130:5; Isaiah 30:18; Lamentations 3:24; and Micah 7:7.

4. He turned from evil and pursued peace. "Turn away from evil and do what is good; / seek peace and pursue it" (Ps. 34:14).

Fear can be caused by sin (evil) that is present in yourself, others, or in some other form near you. Embedded in this verse are four actions: (1) run from the sin you see or sense, which could mean simply getting away from others who are sinning; (2) set your heart and your hands on activities that please the Lord; (3) seek peace by searching for it away from the sin you left behind; and (4) when you find that peace, keep pursuing it and don't look back.

PART 2:
DEALING WITH OPPOSITION FROM WITHIN

Have you ever wondered why Jesus handpicked Judas Iscariot to join the twelve disciples when he knew Judas would betray him? Our Lord had thousands of followers to choose from, yet in his ultimate wisdom he embraced Judas into intimate fellowship—fully knowing his friend would return later with a deathly embrace of his own.

In this tragic story of a misguided follower, what object lessons could Christ be teaching the leaders of his church today? Many leaders experience opposition at certain times in their lives. You could probably rattle off a few disappointments of your own that still leave your head shaking. Opposition is never pleasant. Betrayal can devastate. But Jesus's obvious love of Judas despite the man's evil destiny is an inspiration for us also to love the unlovable. And it's a practical example of God's love for all of us sinful people—even the sinners who jump into ministry careers.

In the rest of this chapter we'll look at how to respond when someone you trust or love opposes you in your ministry calling. Even God's son allowed himself to be betrayed—for our benefit (see Rom. 8:28, 32). So don't be surprised if you go through a similar trial.

Let's say you own a thriving small company that you're sure will grow into an international conglomerate. Would you hire a chief financial officer if you knew he wanted the job in order to commit huge ethical breaches and decimate the very foundation of your business? Would you give this Judas fiduciary responsibility over your entire operation even if you knew he would destroy it?

If you're planning to enter vocational ministry, you may experience a microcosm of this "Judas syndrome." The betrayal probably won't come to a full boil, but resistance, criticism, and ostracism might simmer and bubble from time to time.

UNEXPECTED EARLY OPPOSITION: FAMILY MEMBERS

Your family is one of God's greatest gifts in life and is, therefore, a favorite target for the enemy. Our survey respondents reported that before they started in full-time vocational ministry, their families did one of two things: encouraged or opposed. One crossover leader said, "If your wife is not 110 percent with you, do not do it!"

An obvious challenge comes when all or some of your family members aren't believers. They may not understand your decision and think you're making a major mistake with your life. Their support may be stilted or inconsistent now that you're "churchy."

Family relationships can wilt when church members command your time, attention, and emotional energy—leaving little or nothing at the end of the day for your family. In fact, many of our crossover leaders experienced drastic family upheaval after their ministry began. Relatives felt deserted. Several spent years openly resenting the leader's ministry decision.

In chapter 3 we discussed the importance of sharing your ministry dreams early on with family members. Such open-heart discussions can prevent friction that could undermine

"My family was willing to change addresses and go to a new school, make new friends, etc., all because they knew that God had called. I was off on the dream of my life and they had to endure several years of lifestyle adjustment to a lower salary and a different work schedule."

—Survey respondent

your effectiveness and discourage you. Planning, honesty, and constant communication are the best conflict preventers with your family. If you experience opposition from those closest to you, probe their priorities. Do they believe in God's sovereignty over everything, including and especially your life's work? Also keep in mind the status of the discourager: reservations listed by a believing wife should far outweigh the criticism of a nonbelieving uncle who dismisses your idea out of a lack of understanding, or who believes a career in ministry may be well and good, but it sure doesn't *pay* well and good.

WELCOME TO YOUR NEW FAMILY

Imagine entering a new pastorate. You've completed seminary study, left the workplace behind, and moved your family. Envision feeling more alive than at any time in your life. The pressures of the bottom line, demanding customers, and legal wrangles have been replaced with a passion to live out your true calling and serve God's people. Soon you've got a core group of tireless volunteers creating and running exciting activities and ministries. A few months later your church is sprouting and people are coming to Christ.

Then one of your beloved deacons lands in the hospital, taking him out of commission for a month. Your largest tither moves to a new city, streaking your budget with more red ink than your company ever suffered. A woman you counseled suddenly gets accused of adultery . . . with you.

Strange things happen in full-time ministry leadership—much like in the workplace. I'd like to illuminate this somewhat taboo subject of opposition to set realistic expectations as you consider—or enter—your own new ministry. The church leaders in our study (some with decades of experience feeding their flocks) weren't short on advice and anecdotes about how their sheep have bitten and chewed. Sometimes the sheep drew blood or left scars, but they always taught lessons. A pastor or ministry leader who relies on the Lord in the face of opposition develops character and ultimately matures as a leader (see James 1:2–4).

If you've spent any time in the workplace, you're going to recognize that people are imperfect, no matter where you go—even in the church. The following four types of opposition resonated throughout our research.

But as you read the following drivers of opposition in ministry, remember we serve a God who became human and yet did not sin or lose faith when these flaming arrows flew at him (see Eph. 6:16).

Opposition Driver 1: Change. The American West drew thousands with its promise of riches. People raced to dig up gold, build oil wells, and stick their flags in choice plots of land. This frontier enticed like a slot machine: drop in your money—and uproot your life—for a chance at striking the mother lode. While some found gold, the dreams of the majority delivered only dirt.

The pioneers soon ran out of land to claim, and succeeding generations moved into the industrial age. Fathers were forced to work in factories all day. Then offices became our home away from home. We settled into the groove called the work week, and life developed a sameness most of us know well.

While our forefathers experienced change and discovery on a regular basis, today most people shy away from alterations in their routine. This is especially true in the church, where the mentality of "we've always done it this way, so why change?" runs rampant.

I've got a quirky little habit I can't seem to shake—it's called midday coffee shop visits. I take a sandwich and a laptop and escape the office if only for an hour or two (I happen to be typing in one right now). If I stopped this regular escapade, my life would crumble. I maintain my regular treks to the land of java and come back relaxed and recharged.

"Businesses strive to be responsive to perceived needs and changing market demands or conditions. Churches operate on an entirely different planet." —Survey respondent

Breaking many church members out of their change resistance would be like barring me from my beloved Starbucks. The marketplace-to-ministry leaders in our study long for the days when they instituted change in their businesses with relative ease. Market forces demanded it often. Employees were used to it. In fact, if change didn't occur once in awhile, many got restless.

But when those same workers serve as church volunteers on the weekend, some "refuse to leave the nineteenth century behind," says one respondent. Feelings are easily bruised because of the volunteer mentality, which turns the spotlight on the server rather than the church. The mind-set seems to be, *It's all about how I feel fulfilled as a volunteer, whether my gifts are being used to their fullest, whether I want to devote enough time or feel like volunteering today—not whether I'm contributing to the common goal of the church.*

I understand I'm talking in extremes here, but in my business experience, the goal of making money was clear: if someone detracted from the overall effort, he either changed or left. But plop those malcontents in volunteer roles, and the conflicting issues blossom. Often disagreements or misunderstandings on the collective purpose and vision of the church erupt. Also, ugly dynamics can surface in church and nonprofit boards due to participants protecting turf, defending traditions, and maintaining personal comfort zones. Left to fester, these personal agendas and politicking can conflict with the direction established by the leader—often to the point of derailment and even the church's downfall.

"In the business world it was obvious you had to be willing and able to adapt to the conditions of the marketplace, including current technology and service expectations. This same attitude is almost nonexistent in many churches, especially those who are so deeply entrenched in years of tradition.   — Survey respondent

---

Opposition Driver 2: Control and Authority. The word *kingdom* in the church does not always connote God's territory and rule. I was surprised at the myriad comments in our survey, complaining about the pettiness, immaturity, politics, and backbiting of fellow workers and volunteers. The research reported that many church people try to develop personal kingdoms of influence and power, which contribute to the slow rate of change discussed above. After all, if you ran your own little kingdom and a proposed change threatened to weaken your influence, you'd fight that change, wouldn't you?

In the workplace, money is a means of control and authority. If someone doesn't obey or underperforms, the fear of losing income may hold significant sway over how he or she responds to correction. But if a church volunteer doesn't do his job, the power of the dollar is a nonissue.

"As a social worker, I had the ability, at least in some situations, to simply state how things are going to be. In ministry, the need for consensus, building a supportive group of people for a change, and the time this takes becomes frustrating at times." — Survey respondent

One new church leader who left a high-expectation, highly structured career in the military had trouble adjusting: "Prior to starting our own business, my wife and I were officers in the Air Force. We were accustomed to the concept of taking and giving orders. The church is a much more delicate organization, and the workers are all volunteers. It can be difficult crossing over from an environment where you just tell someone what to do and how you want it done to the church where volunteers must be stroked and coddled."

Many first-time church leaders and staff members struggle with the lack of authority they were used to. Power in the business world can be abused (and often is), but the efficiency of clear lines of command, when executed well, can yield measurable results. The military operates on the same philosophy.

"At first, I was no longer a somebody, and little weight given to my ideas. In the business world, what I said was followed. In the church, people can take it or leave it." — Survey respondent

A different issue arises when these executives enter the ministry world. Power gets diluted or sifts through a strange funnel. Sometimes your authority must be rebuilt entirely. Entrenched staff or church members may feel threatened, distrustful, or doubtful you'll do any better than the last guy in your position. Emotion often overrides decision making based on logic and data. Feeling can supersede rational thinking.

"I had to decide if the Lord was truly calling me into this war zone."
— Survey respondent

Some of the opposition you'll face comes from clashing cultures. If you are motivated by achieving bottom-line results (not necessarily monetary) or are accustomed to straightforward communication and businesslike working relationships, the average church may need awhile to get used to you!

I hasten to defend volunteers, however, by pointing out that they have a challenging balancing act themselves. In addition to serving at the church, many of them juggle full-time jobs, family, church activities, and other volunteer positions. Jumping in their shoes for a moment may open up your perspective on why any given problem has progressed the way it has.

Opposition Driver 3: Conflict and Confrontation. Dr. Glen Martin, a friend, pastor, and experienced church consultant, says, "The devil himself doesn't want the church to succeed." There will be conflict in the church because it is a volunteer organization, but also because it's a big, bright target for a wary, powerful enemy who views the church as his greatest threat on the planet.

"Long-tenured Christians are some of the most difficult to deal with."
— Survey respondent

Conflict is often more personal and difficult to resolve in a church environment. Some respondents report it's even more painful than conflict in the marketplace. One reason may be that day-to-day ministry requires you to deal directly with people's personal lives, whereas in the secular working world, the average personal issue tends to fall under the radar of managers.

One respondent says he was having problems "genuinely having to care about some very difficult people" at church. Maybe he had difficulty getting personal with his new staff. Or maybe it was easier in the business world to treat issues in his subordinates' private lives within the small-talk realm, never letting their difficulties overshadow the company's interests.

The more experience you have in the workplace as a manager, the easier your transition into full-time ministry. Experience in diffusing and mediating conflict will serve you well. If you lack training in conflict management or dealing constructively with confrontation, I urge you to read books or get training in this area.

Another interesting dynamic of church conflict is that staff members, laypeople, and members of the congregation tend to avoid it. An obsessive concern with protecting one another's feelings produces a lot of "dancing," as people dodge issues like a coworker's low performance or a personality conflict. This avoidance bogs down the effectiveness of the overall ministry, keeping important issues and communication from receiving their due.

Opposition Driver 4: Lack of Commitment to Excellence. Winston Churchill said, "I am easily satisfied with the very best." Thankfully, I work with many people who achieve consistent excellence, but they are the exception. In the marketplace I've witnessed apathy, laziness, negativity, and resistance to anything beyond the status quo. People constantly disappoint and fail to rise to the challenge of doing their best.

"As a nursing home administrator with a paid staff, I hired my leadership team, determined and enforced expectations of performance quality, and set deadlines for the completion of projects or reports. As a pastor with a volunteer staff, standards and timeliness of performance is a constant challenge."   —Survey respondent

In the past I've fired people who resisted the company's need for strong leadership in a particular area. I easily measured their performance against goals and quantifiable objectives. When I asked myself if people were getting their assigned jobs done, their negative attitude played a big part in my answer.

Many seasoned church leaders who came from the marketplace bemoan the mediocrity tolerated in so many churches. We should always work as unto the Lord. A quick glance through Proverbs produces a plethora of verses that deal directly with the quality of our work:

The one who is truly lazy in his work
is brother to a vandal. (Prov. 18:9)

A slacker's craving will kill him
because his hands refuse to work. (Prov. 21:25)

Do you see a man skilled in his work?
He will stand in the presence of kings.
He will not stand in the presence of unknown men.
     (Prov. 22:29)

These are strong words indeed. And there are many more verses like this throughout the Bible. God wants us to work hard with skill, excellence, and perseverance—viewing not our earthly supervisors, but *him* as our boss. Why should church staff be allowed to do work that's "good enough"? Shouldn't they be held to the same standard as secular workers?

"At stake in the corporate arena: net profit, return on equity, etc. . . . At stake in the church arena: souls. Which should be more motivating?"

— Survey respondent

Commitment involves more than just excellence, however. In its simplest definition, commitment denotes following through on a pledge or obligation. The wise pastor remembers that volunteers sometimes fail to keep a commitment because of out-of-balance lives or higher priorities that seem worldly or selfish to the observer. Consider the story of Greg Wigfield, who dealt with his own plethora of volunteer difficulties.

LIFESTORY

Greg Wigfield—
From Insurance Agency Owner
to Pastor
Age at crossover: 45
Former position: Entrepreneur/ owner
Company: National Church Group Insurance Agency
Key quote: "I found people questioning whether I could make the move from business into pastoral ministry."

"I started my own business in January 1984. It now generates $15,000,000 per year and employs seventeen people. Both my father and grandfather were full-time, lifelong pastors, so I've been very familiar with ministry issues, but God led me into business.

"In early 1996, I became restless with my life work. Business was successful, but I wanted to do more. During that time, I read two books that had a life-changing effect on my life. The first book, *Halftime* by Bob Buford, started the ball rolling, and Rick Warren's book, *The Purpose-Driven Church*, was the catalyst for change. After reading Warren's book, I flew from my home state of Virginia to California to attend a Purpose-Driven Church seminar hosted by Saddleback Church. While there, I sensed God's call on my life to start a church that focused on reaching people who were unchurched or who had left the church because of irrelevance. My wife was less than enthused about this idea. I began to pray and ask God for confirmation. I also gave my wife veto power over the whole idea. Eventually she encouraged me to follow the dream.

"This began a two-year process of preparation. First, I entered graduate school at Regent University and earned an MA in organizational leadership and divinity. Second, I told a couple of close friends, and we began to pray about God's will and direction in this church plant.

"To make a long story short, I retired from business in 1999 and started Destiny Church in Leesburg, Virginia, in October of that year. We will celebrate our fifth birthday [soon]. The church has not grown as fast as I had hoped. In the beginning, I tried to please many people as I started the church, and this led to trying to please many different agendas. I discovered that the people I was trying to please were churched people, so

I had to make a midcourse correction. This facilitated a mid-course exodus of a significant group of people.

"When I look back on [my decision to please people], I [realize I] would have never done business that way. In business, I focused on the vision, and people chose whether or not to sign up.

"That lesson learned, our church is now doing better than ever. We have a weekly attendance of 250 people, new people are joining us every week, and people are coming to Christ. At least 50 percent of our church is made up of people who have come to Christ under our ministry.

"In the beginning of this transition, I found people questioning whether I could make the move from business into pastoral ministry. To be honest, I questioned it myself. However, I have found it to be a natural transition. I learned much from business that I can apply to ministry. Most important, since I owned my business, I strategized my transition, so that I still receive (and will continue to receive) my full salary from my business. I simply operate as a part-time consultant to the business. This allowed me to start the church without any need of a salary. This has several huge benefits. First, I find it freeing to not be paid from the church—I don't have to worry about the offerings covering my paycheck, and my family's lifestyle did not have to take a dramatic change because of a salary difference. Second, this gave the church extra money to pay other team members as we started the church.

"The story is not over; we have much work to do. However, five years into the project, I can truly say that this is one of the best moves I've ever made."

POINTS TO PONDER

1. How will you handle loneliness or fear?
2. Who is your faithful inner circle right now?
3. Who might be considered your main opposition?

7

||||||||||||||

Looking Back
on a Life of Ministry—
Three Remarkable Stories

It was a long and painful journey.
—SURVEY RESPONDENT

When we asked crossover leaders what their biggest regret was, a large percentage said they had no regrets at all and would do everything again in a second. Some wished they had started sooner. Other interesting regrets include the following:

"I miss close relationships with those in business."

"I felt a call many years earlier and did not respond."

"I did not ask all the critical questions I should have asked, and I did not anticipate the significant differences in how church and business organizations operate."

"I do not interact with as many nonbelieving individuals as with my previous career."

"I loved coaching—two months off in the summer."

"I now have a boss."

"I regret that I did not live out my calling in my previous workplace to the fullest of my ability and God's provision."

"[I regret] not getting it in writing—a contract of sorts. The church promised all these things, and then as time passed, their memory faded."

"I miss the excitement of marketplace evangelism."

I'd like to wrap up with the encouraging stories of three people who led lives of hardship and pain but persevered in their obedience to God's call. The common thread among them is their wisdom of hindsight in recognizing God's hand on every step along the way. Their unexpected twists, turns, and bumps may remind you of your own winding path or that of someone you know. I praise God for these three and the dozens of others who shared their amazing lives with me.

Our first remarkable story is about Ray Bodie, an enthusiastic minister who stepped forward from the crowd of respondents to give me his in-depth personal account. "My story is the reverse," he says. "I left ministry for business. Now, at the age of seventy-five, I have a desire to return to ministry." His unusual journey proves that age has nothing to do with ministry calling. I'll let Mr. Bodie speak for himself:

"After graduating from college and seminary in 1955, I was assigned by the United Methodist Church to a 'vacant lot' in Norfolk, Virginia, to plant a new church.

"It was both an exciting and a welcome challenge. I could not have asked for a better appointment. Starting from scratch was a perfect match for me. I had been married for three years, and we had our first child.

"Meeting in an elementary school, this new church began with two people, my wife and the principal who came to unlock the doors. Three months later, St. John's United Methodist Church was chartered with 154 members, and over the next seven years, the congregation grew to nearly a thousand. When we were appointed to our next church, we were the parents of four children and the new congregation numbered 1,600. My third appointment was as the copastor of a church of 2,800. I was thirty-five.

"To this day, I have never understood the reasoning of being appointed to either the second or third appointments when the first was such a perfect fit. Of course, the official reasoning is that we are a connectional church. So as a faithful UMC minister, I just accepted the next appointment without question.

"I did not recognize the signs right away, but soon I became totally exhausted, burned out, and very depressed. I requested a sabbatical, returned for one more appointment and then requested early retirement as opposed to just leaving, at the age of forty-one.

"I underwent psychological evaluation and medical examinations. Both the tests and counseling indicated that I had the gifts, talents, skills, and calling to be a minister. But I was still plagued with questions, doubts, and unresolved conflicts that were related to the suicidal death of my sister and my leaving St. John's.

"So what would the future be for a former minister of the United Methodist Church with all the skills to be a preacher and pastor, but no training or education for anything else—

with a wife and four children to support? Well, it was very much like entering a new and different universe, learning a new language, and finding your way in the dark or in the wilderness. It was a long and painful journey. Moses became a friend.

"We had no home, no furniture, and no savings. Fortunately, we had no debt. I tried public relations and selling insurance—neither of which I liked or felt that I could spend the rest of my life doing. The Peace Corps was an option, but how could I leave my family?

"Finally, I tried real estate, first sales then management of a real estate office, later becoming a broker, and ultimately becoming the owner. Over a thirty-year period we created a multimillion-dollar investment portfolio. My wife became my business partner. We turned out to be quite a team.

"Our real estate investments are located in six different states and one foreign country. We travel a great deal. Few of our friends, neighbors, or business associates know that I was ever a clergyman. We attend a local United Methodist Church, but I do not sense a vision or a purpose in this two-hundred-year-old congregation. It appears that they have been bypassed by the culture, and the two do not recognize each other.

"I have a desire to reenter the ministry and become a pastor. Do you know of any vacant lot in search of an organizing pastor? By the way, he is seventy-five years of age and may be a bit more mature than [he was at] forty-one. From ministry to business to ministry, quite a reverse, but there just may be a purpose!"

Another gentleman named John Kerce lived a life without regret. A college grad, he joined the Army to chase after the adventure of World War II. After a distinguished career as an officer, he left the service to play professional baseball. But injuries forced the end of his playing days, so he moved behind the mic as a sports radio announcer.

When his family grew, John realized there was better money to be made in business. He got a job as a salesman for Purina and eventually moved into a six-figure management position. But the money, status, and power soon gave way to another bend in the road.

He felt God calling him into ministry, so he enrolled in seminary, ultimately achieving his MA and PhD and accepting a Methodist minister position. During his pastorate he lost his only son in a motorcycle accident—but John's faith stayed strong. His responsibility increased when he assumed the role of district superintendent over many churches. Years later he retired, physically spent and satisfied after a long road of perseverance.

Recently John Kerce looked back on his life from the perspective of its impending end. In the hospital, with the knowledge that he wouldn't live much longer, he started preparing for the biggest change yet—moving to his eternal home. Those close to him were awed by the joyful hymns he sang, by the tearful final meetings he called with friends and family. Here was a man facing death with a song in his heart and without regret. He had run the race. He reassured everyone he saw that dying was not to be feared, and that Jesus's love could not be denied. He knew where he was going and looked forward to reuniting with his wife and son in his true home.

Now that he's gone, his faithful life still reverberates where he lived in the small town of Crestwood, Kentucky. I imagine his story has been told often in sermons by ministers who knew him well. Who couldn't recognize a life so well lived as a gift from God? Who could look at his years on the earth—especially his final weeks—and not be inspired?

We'll end with a lady who found her ministry calling in the last two days of her life.

Renee was a forty-two-year-old mother of three young children who died of cancer after a three-year battle. She and her family showed great courage, strength, and faith before she died. At one point Renee had asked God to heal her and promised to serve him in ministry for as long as she lived. As her illness progressed and the end came into view, she began to wonder what her ministry would've been if God had chosen to heal her. When she was in the ICU in her last days, she asked every person who came into the ward if their life was right with Jesus. Many of the medical staff and visitors were touched by this dying lady and some even brought in their spouses to talk to her.

Renee found the fulfillment of her earthly mission right at the end of her life. But who can measure the results of those few days of ministry? At her funeral three more people committed their lives to the Lord in the midst of a packed hall.

Renee reminds us that it doesn't matter how long our ministry is. Christ himself ministered for only three years. Her story and John Kerce's teach us the importance of leaving a legacy of the love and salvation of Christ, whether we're in a church, the workplace, the mission field, or struggling for survival in a hospital bed.

What legacy will *you* leave? Whatever it is, remember that God can multiply it and take it to new heights long after you're gone. If the Lord calls you into ministry, obey. If he calls you to stay in the workplace, obey and minister to those around you. Wherever he puts you, seek his will for your time there. If that purpose is complete, be sure, and remain sensitive to his next leading. For it is not where we are called, when we are called, or why we are called—it is that we are called to obey.

I pray you will find great joy and true success as you embark on your next great adventure. If you've heard the Lord's call to step out from your current situation, what are you waiting for?

APPENDIX 1:
||||||||||||||

Job Descriptions of Top Ministry Positions

Would it help to see exactly what is expected of church leaders in their job responsibilities? Would reading a detailed job description give you a better picture of what life might be like in the ministry?

A friend of mine named Todd Rhoades created a great site called ChurchStaffing.com that is now owned by Salem Communications. You'll find all kinds of job listings and can post your resume or publish your church's open positions. An area on this site houses sample job descriptions, some of which I've combined into the generic descriptions below. These are meant to convey the flavor of each job, including the tasks, general responsibilities, and education and experience requirements—everything short of salary range, which will depend on the size and budget of the individual church. The churches depicted here are larger than the average church, so you won't find all these positions, like the communications director or missions pastor, at your average small congregation.

I was pleasantly surprised to see that the churches on the site are looking for leaders who practice and exemplify many of the attributes found in this book's research, especially

Thom Rainer's study in chapter 5. The job information summarized below is from churches of several denominations, including Methodist, Southern Baptist, Lutheran, and non-denominational.

SENIOR PASTOR

GENERAL DESCRIPTION AND QUALIFICATIONS

The senior pastor is the chief under-shepherd, vision-caster, preacher, and leader of the church. He is selected for an unspecified period of service by the eldership in conjunction with the personnel council. He will lead, manage, supervise, and minister to the entire staff, leadership, and congregation. He is expected to contribute to the team spirit of the staff through fellowship, encouragement, cooperation, prayer support, and other appropriate ways as he serves his Lord Jesus Christ, the church, and the eldership. He reports directly to the eldership and may or may not be a fellow elder.

Vision casting/team building

The candidate must perform the following activities:

- Buy into the church's vision and be committed to the purpose-driven philosophy
- Be a strong leader who works well with teams
- Have the capacity to envision the future and its possibilities and possess the leadership skills necessary to lead staff, boards, and the church at large
- Spend quality and regular time in receiving and casting vision for the congregation and the church's growth and direction (under the direction of the eldership)

- Be a team player who knows how to surround himself with strong leaders whose gifts augment his own, allowing them the freedom to exercise their gifts
- Be able to communicate and establish effective working relationships with many different people
- Be able to work under stress and cope with multiple and varied issues
- Possess solid time-management skills and organizational abilities, able to coordinate several activities at once and quickly analyze and resolve specific problems
- Create goal ownership and a sense of shared purpose among the laity through leading by example, involving others in the decision-making process, and actively participating in meetings and events
- Evaluate growth and development strategies for effectiveness in achieving goals

Communication

The senior pastor will be the primary spiritual leader and communicator of the church's vision to staff, congregation (members, attendees, seekers), and the community at large, so he must be able to perform the following:

- Present or provide the spiritual information necessary for believers in all stages of maturity to develop into faithful, devoted followers of Jesus Christ
- Be responsible for the preaching ministry of the church, clearing all guest and staff preachers and their preaching
- Lead the congregation in vibrant worship services, making the gospel relevant to people's lives through clarity in preaching and communicating a comprehensive understanding of the Bible and Christian theology

- Strive to develop preaching and teaching methods that will inspire and challenge spiritual growth of the congregation and will have the capacity to make the gospel attractive to visitors
- Create and deliver messages that demonstrate that Jesus brings help for this life and hope for the future
- Be an effective catalyst for change in his audiences through information and inspiration as opposed to condemnation
- Be a good communicator and be able to work with a variety of presentation forms
- Be able to (1) read, analyze, and interpret the most complex documents, (2) respond effectively to the most sensitive inquiries or complaints, (3) write speeches and articles using original or innovative techniques or style, and (4) make effective and persuasive presentations on controversial or complex topics to top management, public groups, and/or boards of directors
- Possess a mind that is open to new ideas and to giving them a fair trial
- Adjust to new situations, seek new ideas and opportunities for change, and be flexible and adaptable
- Use sound judgment and make solid decisions based on assessment of facts
- Be flexible, friendly, approachable, and honest, dealing with conflict directly, openly, honestly, and graciously

Personal walk

The senior pastor must have a vibrant, intimate, personal relationship with Jesus and a passion for the unchurched and hurting people of the community. He must exhibit a passion for God and a Christlike spirit. These qualities will be evidenced in his personal life, his family relationships, and his ministry. He nurtures his inner self through a disciplined life of daily fellowship with God in prayer and Bible study. Specifically, he performs the following:

- Meets the scriptural requirements for an elder
- Sets aside quality, adequate time for study that prepares him for teaching and preaching
- Spends approximately thirty minutes in prayer and one hour in study of God's Word on a daily basis
- Engages in consistent daily memorization of Scripture
- Sets aside two to three hours per week for calling, recruiting, and training others to make evangelistic calls
- Participates in personal discipleship, either in a small group or one-on-one
- Spends one day a month in prayer and fasting
- Stays current with the trends of his ministry by listening to tapes, reading books and periodicals, and attending approved conferences

EDUCATION/EXPERIENCE

The senior pastor should have a Master of Divinity degree or equivalent or four to ten years' related experience and/or training or an equivalent combination of education and experience.

ADDITIONAL DUTIES

The senior pastor will perform the following duties:

- Systematically train disciples and equip leaders for ministry through personal modeling, mentoring, and programming

- Conduct new membership classes for those interested in joining the church and instruct people who seek conversion to faith
- Conduct weddings and funeral services and perform baby dedications and baptisms
- Visit people in the midst of crises (i.e., death, sickness, trauma, or other significant events), where pastoral care is required, demonstrating warmth, openness, and sensitivity to the needs of those involved
- Counsel those in spiritual need and comfort the bereaved, assisting those facing problems or decisions
- Oversee all religious education programs to ensure programs and curriculum are in keeping with the overall goals and philosophy of the church
- Guide the church members to responsible biblical giving through stewardship development
- Is responsible for the implementation of strategies to reach the unchurched and to grow faithful, devoted followers of Jesus Christ
- Is in ultimate charge of the church's worship services, delegating the planning and leading of the services to the music pastor in conjunction with the executive pastor
- Is responsible for the staff, delegating to the executive pastor the responsibility of supervising the staff. In conjunction with the executive pastor, will make appropriate recommendations for hiring and dismissals
- Meets regularly with the personnel/administrative council for input and chairs and meets regularly with that council (made up of his executive pastor, chairman of the elders, vice president of the elders, elder representative, and controller)

- Report to and maintain a very close liaison with the eldership, meeting with them regularly on a formal and informal basis, usually twice monthly.
- Do outside speaking and attend appropriate functions that will enhance the church's growth with the approval of the eldership.

EXECUTIVE PASTOR

GENERAL DESCRIPTION AND QUALIFICATIONS

The role of the executive pastor (EP) is to assist the elders and the senior pastor in overseeing the life and direction of the church. This will require a firm grasp of the purpose, values, and strategy of the church and the ability to align staff and key leadership teams with its mission. The EP will offer pastoral leadership to the congregation alongside and, when necessary, in place of the senior pastor. He will ensure that the systems, practices, and policies of the church responsibly and effectively support its ministry activities. His main focus is working with the leadership team to implement the vision of the senior pastor and elders. He is expected to contribute to the team spirit of the staff through fellowship, encouragement, cooperation, prayer support, and other appropriate ways as he serves his Lord Jesus Christ, the church, and the senior pastor.

Strategic planning/leadership

The EP is responsible for strategic planning and staff coordination in the execution of the church's purpose. He will define strategic goals and vision as a key leader among staff and elders. He will provide the catalyzing challenges and activities to the staff and elders, allowing them to remain true to their purpose, and develop new ministry programs, helping staff and elders be appropriately responsive to identified needs and church growth. This leadership and input will be provided through the following activities:

- Coordinating and leading weekly staff meetings and other activities designed to clarify and execute the church's goals and objectives
- Serving as an elder and primary staff liaison to elders and providing leadership in vision casting and goal setting
- Monitoring the pulse of the congregation through research and evaluation
- Ensuring that staffing, facilities, and programs are appropriately and effectively aligned to best meet strategic goals
- Serving as a proven leader and strategic thinker who will guide the pastoral staff in casting vision and mobilize administrative support to maintain and advance the ministry of the church
- Ensuring effective consensus building and decision making among the staff teams
- Exhibiting strong interpersonal skills, showing the ability to communicate persuasively and compassionately both orally and in writing
- Teaching and preaching as needed, though this skill is not a requirement for the job
- Assisting the pastoral staff in goal setting, planning, prioritizing, and ministry implementation

Personnel and administration

He will serve as chief of staff and personnel director for pastors, paid staff, and lay volunteers. The EP will lead, evaluate, and mentor existing staff in their respective areas of ministry and prioritize staff additions. Specifically, he will perform the following functions:

- Oversee training and development for the pastoral staff
- Hire and dismiss staff after consultation and guidance from the elders, conducting all "new hire" and "exit" interviews with members of the pastoral staff
- Provide leadership to the pastoral staff in the design and implementation of all church ministries
- Work with the personnel team to implement salary reviews and recommendations
- Maintain efficient and effective lines of communication between the staff and elders
- Serve as human resources manager, overseeing the negotiation of insurance and other benefits, conducting performance evaluations, and providing ongoing informal performance feedback
- Oversee and execute the administration of the church through appropriate staff, lay leadership teams, and consultants (as needed and approved by the elders), ensuring the completion of business, facility, and logistical support functions through staff and lay volunteers
- Serve as the chief financial officer, providing oversight and direction in the financial functions of the church and managing fund-raising, cash flow, contributions, insurance, banking and financing, payroll, leases, budget planning and oversight (and can review and correct errors in budget reports)
- Recruit, train, and manage staff or laypeople to perform budgeting and administrative responsibilities

- Supervise the office manager and provide direction, as needed, for the effective functioning of the front office support functions
- Oversee the effective functioning and maintenance of computer, information, and communication systems with support from lay volunteers and paid tech consultants
- Oversee development of and adherence to church policies and procedures
- Develop a strong biblical foundation for wise management in a church setting, establishing and maintaining appropriate standards for the accomplishment of ministry in a way that honors both God and people
- Serve as a member of the administrative council, working closely with the senior pastor to develop agendas and report on staff and ministry-related issues as appropriate
- Work with the senior pastor to maintain and protect the senior pastor's schedule
- Chair the committee that approves the senior pastor's outside speaking engagements
- Coordinate and approve vacation dates for all pastoral staff
- Maintain up-to-date job descriptions for all pastoral staff
- Make recommendations to the senior pastor and administrative council regarding salary increases for pastoral staff
- Project future staff needs, making recommendations regarding staff additions or changes in ministry responsibilities

- Oversee the church advertising and marketing for worship services
- With the senior pastor, set agenda for staff/elder retreats, planning retreats, and all-day team leader meetings
- Coordinate and organize all Bible conferences, pastors' conferences, nonmusical special events, elder/staff retreats, and planning retreats
- Provide direct oversight for capital stewardship campaigns
- Oversee the development, implementation, and continued monitoring of each departmental budget to ensure that each ministry is budgeting for growth
- With the controller, manage revenue projections and expenditures
- Approve all ministry expenses
- Supervise the position of controller, facility manager, and all team leaders. Is administratively responsible for all staff
- Meet as needed with all staff personnel under his direct supervision to provide support, encouragement, training, accountability, and direction in their ministries
- Maintain strong accountability with staff in all areas of ministry for growth spiritually, numerically, and evangelistically
- Conduct a six-month evaluation of all staff members reporting directly to him and review all evaluations with the pastoral staff once a year in a one-on-one setting
- Assist each staff person in functioning at a high level of proficiency

- Make a recommendation to staff regarding training conferences and approve all conferences to be attended by pastoral staff
- Establish performance goals for his ministry and implement strategies for their attainment through the power and direction of the Holy Spirit
- Work with each staff member on his team to maintain a balanced work schedule, keeping track of vacation days, sick days, days off, make-up days, personal days, etc.
- Schedule the pastors and interns for Wednesday night services, special events/productions, membership class presentations, and custodial devotions, disseminating schedules in a timely and efficient manner

Publicity/marketing

The EP's responsibilities in promoting include the following:

- Develop, edit, and proof the monthly newsletter and weekly bulletin, working with the staff and graphics department to present a high-quality, accurate, timely information piece for the congregation and community
- Develop and maintain newspaper advertising, phone advertising, and special mailings to the congregation
- Approve all content and make recommendations for the church's Web site
- Serve as spokesman for the church on all print, radio, and television media requests for comment in non-crisis situations

EDUCATION/EXPERIENCE

The EP will have the following education and experience:

- Bachelor's degree in business administration, public administration, religion/Bible, or related field (master's seminary degree is preferred)
- Five or more years' experience managing a million-dollar-plus church or corporation
- Five or more years leading within a church setting—able to understand, motivate, and support ministry leaders (the ideal candidate will have experience supervising and mentoring pastoral staff)
- Proven skills in change management, visioneering, conflict, and people management
- Proven experience in mobilizing and raising lay volunteers and leadership
- Biblical qualifications outlined in 1 Timothy 3

MISSION COORDINATOR OR MISSIONS PASTOR

GENERAL DESCRIPTION AND QUALIFICATIONS

He or she will work with the pastor, paid and volunteer staff, membership, and other sources in coordinating and supporting a comprehensive churchwide missions ministry that keeps with the overall purpose and values of the church. Specifically, the mission coordinator/pastor will have the following attributes:

- Team oriented with the ability to design, implement, and mature a missions ministry that honors our Lord

- Skilled in personal evangelism and soul winning
- Passionate about missions and possessing practical international mission experience as well as team and leadership skills
- Organized and diplomatic with training and development skills
- Experienced in financial planning and management and program development and execution
- Skilled in computer capabilities, specifically in Microsoft Office and church software
- Highly ethical and able to process highly sensitive information
- Action and goal oriented
- Excelling in ministry commitment, conduct, and professionalism
- Flexible—able to change and work in a dynamic, growth-oriented environment where the objectives are emerging and not clearly defined
- Able to relate well to missionaries and their needs as well as missions organizations and their expectations
- Able to develop and implement a missions program strategy
- Able to administer programs and detail work well
- Supportive of the traditional evangelical theology for which the church stands

DUTIES AND RESPONSIBILITIES

The missions coordinator/pastor will plan, coordinate, administer, and evaluate a comprehensive mission education program through the missions council. He or she will develop a clear vision and goals for local, state, national, and foreign mission encounters. Specifically, the coordinator/pastor will perform the following duties:

- Establish and maintain exciting and effective communications about missions with the staff and church at large
- Serve as the church liaison to the missions committee, relating directly, as needed, with the directors of local social ministries. May coordinate complementary ministries such as counseling and crisis recovery
- Organize mission trips for the church, providing candid follow-up evaluation, including an assessment of the short- and long-term success and impact of each mission encounter
- With the mission committee, develop policies, goals, and an operating philosophy for the missions ministry for approval by the pastor, acting as the primary resource person for mission information throughout the church
- Manage the day-to-day and long-range financial, administrative, and human resource aspects of the missions ministry
- Develop effective communications with staff, volunteers, and potential volunteers
- Ensure that appropriate safety and security measures are in place, particularly in international travel
- Give overall direction to the missions program and emphasis of the church
- Lead in the design and implementation of the church's missions program

- Relate directly to the church-supported missionaries, seeking to relate them to the church family and assist in addressing their needs and concerns
- Give counsel to present and potential missionaries
- Integrate missions awareness and education into the life of the church

EDUCATION/EXPERIENCE

For this position, a bachelor's and divinity degree are desirable, along with at least five years' experience in relating to missions organizations and missionaries.

YOUTH PASTOR

GENERAL DESCRIPTION, QUALIFICATIONS, DUTIES

The first priority of the youth pastor is to be involved in teens' lives—establishing relationships with them, shepherding them, and helping them develop their own relationship with Jesus Christ. These relationships will be built by attending the teens' ball games, recitals, lunches, and other activities. The youth pastor organizes activities of the junior/senior high students that will promote an environment for the development of socially rounded, spiritually superior young adults. The youth pastor shall provide feedback to parents concerning spiritual growth and/or disciplinary issues with their teens. The youth pastor shall attend all church outreaches in the community as youth representative and travel with youth on events and outings. The youth pastor shall have proven interpersonal and conflict management skills. He shall work to develop an environment of unity and community in the youth ministry. The youth pastor's specific duties include the following:

- Assist the leadership team in defining the vision for the spiritual development of the junior and senior high youth ministry
- Provide regular reports to the leadership team concerning the status of the youth ministry and identifying successes and problems to be addressed
- Establish and maintain policies concerning operation of the youth ministry
- Oversee Christian education for senior and junior high Sunday school and the area Bible study ministry
- Establish and maintain an adult youth staff—comprised of interested and motivated parents/adults—that meets regularly (and preside over the meetings)
- Recruit volunteers to participate in and lead various programs and teaching and service activities
- Attend ministry team meetings to update progress of ministry and present an annual report to church chairman for the annual meeting
- Develop and follow an annual budget for the youth ministry, maintain current medical files and parental release forms, oversee fund-raising related to various activities, and supervise the support and operation of the teen center
- Encourage youth to develop leadership abilities and participate in the daily workings of the church
- Acknowledge youth as part of the total church family, seizing opportunities to develop the youth program within the present structures of the parish
- Develop a core support group of youth, youth executives, and volunteers

- Plan, arrange, and coordinate (1) one youth event per month for grades five and six, (2) two junior high/senior high events per month, and (3) one college and career event per month
- Teach, plan, and coordinate a weekly confirmation program—involving parents in the program as snack/potluck and advent/closing potluck providers—organizing an initial information meeting of program and confirmation celebrations (weekend/workshop/banquet)
- Produce bulletin announcements on youth news and help with bulletin board management
- Gather parent/guardian information updates
- Provide support for Sunday school superintendent/program/curriculum
- Assist at vacation Bible camp

Business Administrator

GENERAL DESCRIPTION, QUALIFICATIONS, AND DUTIES

The business administrator will support the pastor in the administration of the business functions of the church, working closely with the deacons and eldership. This minister is the steward of the physical, financial, and personnel resources of the church.

The business administrator's qualifications include the following:

- Organizational/administrative skills
- Business and accounting background/education
- People skills

- Verbal and written communication skills
- Discretion
- Integrity
- Persistence in developing skills/knowledge

Personnel

The business administrator will act as administrative staff liaison between pastoral staff, pastor, and leadership team, specifically performing the following duties:

- Recruit, interview, hire, train, supervise, evaluate, and terminate support staff—including secretarial, maintenance, and janitorial—in consultation with the senior pastor
- Oversee contracted personnel and special service personnel
- Maintain current job descriptions for all staff members
- Conduct verbal and written job performance discussions with the support staff annually
- Attend to circumstances where support staff performance is less than satisfactory
- Schedule hourly staff work hours and approve/disapprove overtime
- Maintain personnel files and time reporting records
- Coordinate volunteers as necessary
- Supervise the manager of church facilities and accounting/finance staff
- Give direction as needed for organization and development of other office staff and volunteers
- Conduct periodic formal performance evaluations and assist in setting goals
- Provide direction to the accounting/finance staff as needed

- Supervise receptionists and provide direction as needed
- Supervise the database administrator

Office Management

The business administrator will plan, direct, and guide the church office's work, performing the following specific duties:

- Develop and implement an efficient and effective office organization by improving methods and procedures
- Assure adequate inventory of equipment and supplies
- Maintain and update calendar of events and room schedules
- Assess needs of congregation to ensure office hours are serving those needs
- Develop sufficient backup plans for staff coverage due to vacations, illness, etc.
- Supervise the purchase of furniture, computers, and office equipment
- Oversee all church insurance policies, acquisitions, and claims reporting
- Work with staff and committee chairpersons to determine equipment needs
- Work with staff, committees, and other lay leadership to establish and implement church policies as directed by the executive pastor
- Maintain files of all legal documents of the church
- Attend annual training seminars/courses

Financial Administration

The business administrator will assist in identifying budget line-item overages, determining causes, and developing financial policies to assure proper adherence, performing the following functions:

- Ensure Sunday morning collection procedures are clear and secure
- Ensure banking operations are managed properly
- Serve as a central purchasing agent for office supplies and equipment, performing price comparisons, securing bids, preparing proposals, and providing recommendations to trustees for large purchases
- Plan and oversee the building and administrative budget accounts, equipment acquisitions, and building/maintenance budgets
- Assist the executive pastor and/or staff parish relations committee in preparing the personnel budget
- Assist staff and committee chairpersons in budget preparation and account maintenance
- Oversee annual budget preparation for review by the finance committee and assist in presentations
- Provide stewardship committee with financial information, as requested
- Present financial reports at finance committee, planned giving committees, board of trustees, and administrative council meetings
- Develop and oversee implementation of financial policies, procedures, and reporting
- Advise the church treasurer of the current financial status of the church
- Perform monthly bank reconciliations
- Prepare monthly financial statements, including adjusting journal entries
- Represent church legally to establish bank and investment accounts, make investments, and withdraw or transfer funds as needed

- Work with the certified public accountant during the annual audit
- Process semimonthly payroll and any special payrolls
- Review and maintain necessary computer payroll reports
- Maintain individual employee payroll files
- Communicate and administer employee benefit packages
- Distribute W-4s and I-9s and review and distribute annual W-2s and 1099s

Membership Management

The business administrator will perform duties of a church clerk as outlined in the bylaws, performing the following functions:

- Track those who attend and their status in the membership process
- Coordinate with senior pastor on scheduling classes
- Coordinate with deacons on hearing of testimonies
- Coordinate with parish pastor and deaconesses on baptisms
- Coordinate with church moderator on voting of new members
- Coordinate with staff on recognition of new members during worship services
- Coordinate with parish pastor on newcomers' socials
- Ensure maintenance of Membership Plus database, including production of reports as required to update the status of members, ABF groups, spiritual gifts/talents, and other census information

Building and Grounds

The business administrator will manage scheduling and use of the building and facilities, performing the following functions:

- Ensure development of maintenance and replacement schedules, overseeing security and maintenance of grounds
- Oversee grounds volunteers
- Oversee scheduling, maintenance, and use of church vans

Communication/Publishing

The business administrator will serve as editor of church publications including, but not limited to, weekly bulletins, monthly newsletters, board minutes, annual reports, flyers, inserts, missions brochures, program guides, devotional booklets, etc. He/she will also attend quarterly and special business meetings and publish their minutes.

Communications Director

GENERAL DESCRIPTION AND DUTIES

The communications director will work under the supervision of the executive pastor on external/internal communications and marketing issues with the primary directive to evangelize our community (and world) and be used by God to help facilitate growth of the church family. This person will also provide creative counsel and direction for the music pastor, the creative arts director, and others as they organize and produce outreach events and the weekly worship services. This person will be expected to contribute to the team spirit of the staff through fellowship, encouragement, cooperation, prayer, and other appropriate ways as he/she serves the Lord Jesus Christ and the church family. The director will perform the following functions:

- Provide leadership and management in the area of external/internal communications and marketing through print and electronic means
- Provide creative leadership and direction with regard to major outreach events and weekly worship services
- Provide creative and marketing counsel for other church ministries and organizations as they seek to effectively reach specific people groups
- Nurture the participants/volunteers in this ministry toward Christlikeness and the fulfillment of the Great Commission
- Become a member of the church and attend services regularly
- Have a growing walk with Christ, exemplified by a life of obedience and example
- Be current on creative communication and technological trends (by reviewing tapes, reading books and periodicals, and attending approved events) and look for opportunities to use this information to more effectively communicate with the community and church
- Direct the external communications of the church (including broadcast, print, direct mail, Internet, and opinion leader contacts), "marketing" the church through effective positioning and branding within the community, nation, and world
- Direct the internal communications of the church (including improving communication between the

staff and church family; updating interpersonal/interoffice communication by establishing protocols for effective e-mail, messaging, voice mail, and Intranet development and usage; and managing the receptionist corps, as well as signage in and around the property)

- Supervise the publications and printing process by overseeing the graphics and print departments (for the weekly church bulletin, visitor information, and all other mass publications)
- Oversee the external advertising/communications/marketing of the church
- Oversee the creation and management of the church's Web site and seek new technologies and opportunities to improve the effectiveness of Web-related communication
- Work in cooperation, and ultimately oversee, the information services/technology department to ensure the church's electronic/Web-based communication is functional and database information is readily available
- Serve as the media/community-relations liaison and be the primary interface with the news media and other mass communications outlets, strengthening media relationships and effectively reaching community/opinion leaders
- Serve as communications counsel to church staff with regard to media and public inquiries
- Oversee all external communication (print, broadcast, direct mail, etc.) to the community at large. Build volunteer teams of creative professionals to help counsel

and direct the overall communications, marketing, and creative effort

- Serve as creative/communications/marketing counselor for other church ministries and organizations as they seek to effectively reach and communicate with specific people groups
- Serve a primary role in cooperation with the music pastor and others with regard to the creative development and implementation of outreach events and all church services
- Attend weekly staff meetings

APPENDIX 2:
|||||||||||||||

The Church Consulting Field

"Ninety-four percent of churches [are] either in decline or growing at a slower rate than the communities in which they serve."

–THOM RAINER

If you're not ready to jump into the full-time ministry fray, an excellent option to explore is church consulting.

We've trained more than nine hundred leaders through Church Central's five-level program. Most of them haven't gone on to full-time careers in the field. Many are pastors who want to help their church and others in the community. Some are retirees. One gentleman with decades of ministry experience says, "I just want to help one more church before I go."

A desperate need exists for more experienced, trained consultants. The majority of today's churches don't know how to break free from mediocrity. The need for outside help has never been greater. Unfortunately, many churches close their minds to enlisting the aid of a consultant because they don't think they have problems or they don't know what a consultant can do for them—daunting obstacles indeed.

Let's look at the basics of the field and how the process works. We'll finish with a self-assessment quiz to help you determine if you're cut from consulting cloth.

CHURCH CONSULTING 101

The typical consultation begins with a clear goal of analyzing existing conditions in a church and suggesting improvements for its overall health. In the process, a qualified consultant, who is not a member of the church, provides insight and recommendations to improve the church's functions in light of God's specific purposes for all churches as described in Acts 2:42–47 (Rick Warren's *The Purpose-Driven Church* is the classic work on this topic).

The idea of church *growth* is often related to numbers—the number of new members, persons baptized into the church, and other statistics. Church *health* is related to how well the body of Christ functions in terms of fulfilling God's mission and purpose.

Healthy churches are most effective when the six purposes of Acts 2:42–47 are intentional, active, and balanced:

1. fellowship
2. worship
3. ministry

4. discipleship
5. evangelism
6. prayer

Based on the goals of the church, consultants perform one or more of the following services when called on by church leaders:

- listen
- recommend
- analyze

- investigate
- encourage change
- help implement change, when needed

Consultations vary in terms of their focus and intensity. Most focus on specific areas of church health, though a comprehensive consultation is desirable. This full-service engagement focuses on the following areas:

1. Finance
2. Planning/goal setting
3. Growth barriers
4. Outreach/evangelistic approaches
5. Community analysis
6. Mission/vision
7. Assimilation effectiveness
8. Perceptions/attitudes toward the church among attendees
9. Data and statistical analysis
10. Small group/Sunday school
11. Worship issues
12. Leadership effectiveness
13. Prayer emphasis
14. Missions
15. Personnel issues
16. Programming/ministries analysis
17. Facilities analysis
18. Denominational issues
19. Ministry staff alignment

Church consultation services may vary widely, though the most effective church consultants include each of the following steps in their work (in sequential order):

1. Consultation request
2. Initial interview
3. Proposal to church leadership
4. Acceptance

5. Consultation work
6. Initial verbal report to leadership
7. Written report (presented to the senior pastor first)
8. Final report
9. Presentation to church leadership
10. If needed, proposal for future action
11. Follow-up

When exploring church consultation, the pastor and leaders should discuss the experience and qualities of the consultant. The following are questions you may encounter if you're being considered for consulting:

- Do you have experience with our denomination?
- To what degree do you have experience with churches of our size and life stage?
- What is your specific interest in working with our church?

Church leaders will want to know you have the maturity and attitude needed to work effectively with them. They'll assess your ability and style in speaking and writing.

No official code of ethics exists for church consultants. However, the following is the code Church Central's trained and/or licensed consultants agree to.

The Church Consultant's Code of Ethics:

- As a church consultant I will work under the Lordship of Jesus Christ and hold to the authority of the Bible;
- be honest and not knowingly misrepresent facts;
- divulge any potential conflicts of interest as soon as they are known;
- only accept projects that can be completed in a professional and timely manner;
- safeguard any confidential information or documents;

- not divulge any confidential information without the consent of the church/client;
- abide by all applicable local, county, state, and federal laws;
- report all time worked and expenses incurred accurately and honestly; and
- meet all requirements to maintain my integrity as a certified consultant.

WHY CHURCHES USE CONSULTANTS

An analysis of the seven-hundred-plus church consultation requests Dr. Rainer's group received over a five-year period reveals both *reactive* and *proactive* reasons that church leaders seek qualified, external consultants.

Typically a senior pastor or minister (or a person calling on his behalf) contacts a consultant with questions about a specific issue—usually a painful one—within the church. The chief problems and reactive reasons for seeking a consultation are as follows:

- Attendance has plateaued or declined.
- Planned giving and/or offerings are declining.
- Persons attending do not return or join the church.
- Conflict exists within the church between pastoral leadership and lay leadership or between groups of laity.

Consultation requests based on a desire to *proactively* address the church's health and growth fall into three primary areas:

- The church does not have a plan for ensuring its growth either short-term and/or long-term, and wants to have a plan.

- The church desires to start a major effort in its life and ministry, such as a building expansion, mission effort, capital campaign, etc.
- The church is doing OK but is not sure what its strengths and weaknesses are.

In a two-year period, the number of consultation requests more than doubled. Why? The Rainer team discovered that the church leaders requesting the consultation were focused on speedy, but thorough, solutions to church problems and goals, and consultants could assess and address issues more quickly than church staff. More than likely, this trend will continue.

AM I CUT OUT FOR CHURCH CONSULTING?

The following quiz will give you some perspective on your readiness for entering this field.

1. Do you have more than five years' experience serving on a church staff?

    Yes _____   No _____

2. Do you understand how a church can be unhealthy?

    Yes _____   No _____

3. Do you feel a deep desire to help churches become healthy?

    Yes _____   No _____

4. Do you currently have an adequate source of income?

    Yes _____   No _____

5. Do you have any experience in the business world?

    Yes _____   No _____

6. Do you know of at least three churches that are significantly unhealthy?

    Yes _____   No _____

7. Have you ever been involved in resolving serious church conflict?

Yes _____   No _____

(Give yourself one point for every *yes* then find your score below.)

SCORE: 6-7

You have the highest *chance of success if you decide to pursue church consulting.* You have the experience, desire, and opportunity necessary to help struggling churches. You are a natural candidate for professional training. Give yourself a chance to try out consulting. Pray for and seek a trial run at this endeavor. You may eventually consider establishing a consulting business after a time of trying it out. But if you're between jobs, don't jump into consulting as a primary source of income.

SCORE: 4-5

You have a good *chance of success if you decide to pursue church consulting.* If you scored in this range, you should *not* consider becoming a full-time consultant, but you still have what it takes to revitalize churches. If you work at it, you'll secure some paid consultations, but don't limit yourself to doing only those. You have some qualities that can and should be put to use in churches, regardless of their ability to pay. Investigate various resources and training to equip you for this work.

SCORE: 0-3

You have a modest to low *chance of success if you decide to pursue consulting.* As you evaluate your next steps in ministry and life, consider focusing your time, efforts, and resources on your home church rather than others. Investing your talents in your own congregation will probably be more fruitful because you know the people, issues, and opportunities in an intimate way. Consultant training can refine your skills, but your main goal should be to support your church's leadership and laity in every way you can. Remember—the best leaders have the best teams behind them.

No matter what you scored, remember to pray. Listen for the Lord's leading. Search the Scriptures. Talk to pastors and other church consultants. And take stock of what you really expect out of your consulting efforts. If your main goal is income, you are likely to be disappointed for awhile. Make sure you can support yourself while you build your clientele.

True success is measured by the churches you help. The best consultant candidates have an insatiable desire to glorify Christ and see his church expand on the earth.

APPENDIX 3:
IIIIIIIIIIIIIII

Recommended Books and Web Sites

I pray the following resources will prove helpful to you as you investigate becoming a ministry professional.

BOOKS

The Dream Giver—Bruce Wilkinson (Multnomah, 2003). This parable begins with the story of Ordinary, who dares to leave the Land of Familiar to pursue his Big Dream. With the help of the Dream Giver, Ordinary begins the hardest and most rewarding journey of his life. Wilkinson gives readers practical, biblical keys to fulfilling their own dreams, revealing that there's no limit to what God can accomplish when we choose to pursue the dreams he gives us for his honor.

Living Your Heart's Desire: God's Call and Your Vocation—Gregory S. Clapper (Upper Room Books, 2005). This book helps people who are struggling to align their faith and their work, clarifying what it means to have a calling from God and how to live it out. By presenting some of the key features of the Christian truth of God's call, this book can help Christians lead fulfilled and joyful lives, regardless of how they make money.

From Success to Significance—Lloyd Reeb (Zondervan, 2004). You'll get encouragement and practical advice on how to infuse significance into the second half of your life, without having to achieve financial independence or abandon your first-half career.

The Life You've Always Wanted—John Ortberg (Zondervan, 2002). Ortberg says God isn't only concerned with our spiritual lives but wants to impact every aspect of ordinary living. This book explores life beyond performance and externalism into the realm of joy, peace, kindness, and a growing faith.

Made to Count: Discovering What to Do with Your Life—Bob Reccord and Randy Singer (W Publishing Group, 2004). Rarely have we heard a pastor urge us to seek our call in the secular marketplace or to impact the world by raising godly children. The authors discuss how God calls people to the most surprising places and unlikely professions for the purpose of changing our world.

Don't Waste Your Life—John Piper (Crossway Books, 2004). Piper calls younger generations to make their lives count for eternity, braving the risks to achieve the rewards. Readers will find their passion for the cross of Christ enlarged.

Sorting It Out: Discerning God's Call to Ministry—Alice R. Cullinan (Judson Press, 1999). This book walks Christians of all ages and experiences through the questions and uncertainties that come with a person's call to vocational ministry. It's very different from mine and might be a good complement if you'd like to continue researching this field.

Is It I, Lord?—James O. Chatham (Westminster John Knox Press, 2002). Another complementary read from a denominational viewpoint.

Jesus, Life Coach: Learn from the Best—Laurie Beth Jones (Thomas Nelson Inc., 2004). Delving into the principles Jesus used to transform those around him, this book offers proven strategies and applications for navigating the path ahead.

Your Best Life Now: 7 Steps to Living at Your Full Potential—Joel Osteen (Warner Faith, 2004). Houston televangelist Joel Osteen says that achieving a successful, prosperous life of fulfillment can only occur when we stop worrying about the past or future. He exhorts us to make the most of each present moment by using our God-given strengths and talents to achieve our goals.

The Journey from Success to Significance—John Maxwell (J. Countryman, 2004). Maxwell looks beyond a worldly view of what matters to find a deeper call and a greater purpose in life. Stripping away the myths of success touted by our culture, he asserts that true significance is only found by living in relationship with God and by using one's energy and influence to pass along God's love to others.

Finishing Well—Bob Buford (Integrity Publishers, 2004). "Twenty years from now," Buford writes, "the rules for this second adulthood as a productive season of life may be better known. But for now, we're out across the frontier breaking new ground." Buford sits you at the feet of sixty leaders who have achieved significance beyond their impressive success in life. He explains how you can shift into a far more fulfilling life now, no matter your age.

Halftime—Bob Buford (Zondervan, 1997). In this classic title that inspired an entire genre of "significance" books, Buford says broaching midlife doesn't have to be a crisis. In fact, he insists that it is actually an opportunity to begin the better half of life. Buford argues that whether you are a millionaire, a manager, or a teacher, you will one day have to transition from the struggle for success to the quest for significance.

WEB SITES

www.halftime.org—Sign up for Bob Buford's *Halftime Report*, a free monthly newsletter.

www.ACTIVEenergy.net—Another great newsletter, which Buford calls his "personal musings," is available on this site.

www.ChurchCentral.com—Learn more about church consultant training; the site "equips leaders to grow healthier churches."

www.leadlikejesus.com—An initiative started by Ken Blanchard and Phil Hodges to encourage business leaders to use Jesus as their coach for developing leadership skills.

www.ChurchStaffing.com—A leading source of information for churches and church staff members in the area of personnel and staff relations.

APPENDIX 4:
||||||||||||

The Marketplace-
to-Ministry Survey

This appendix covers the results of our survey. First, a few quick facts to explain its background:

- The survey included 344 respondents.
- While not large enough to be scientifically valid, its statistical accuracy falls into the threshold of +/- 5 percent.
- The target survey list includes subscribers to *Church Health Today*, a free e-mail newsletter published by Church Central.
- The subscribers were supplemented by an e-mail list of pastors acquired by Church Central from an outside source.

The following list of questions and answers make up the entire body of objective data upon which this book was based. The subjective responses appear throughout the book, and were culled from more than one thousand individual, and sometimes lengthy, comments.

1. In what type of ministry position do you currently serve?

Full-time pastor/minister	46.5%	(160)
Part-time (or "bivocational") pastor/minister	10.8%	(37)
Full- or part-time student	4.1%	(14)
Parachurch/nonprofit	9.9%	(34)
Church staff member	14.5%	(50)
Full-time missionary	1.5%	(5)
Volunteer church lay leader	5.2%	(18)
Professor/teacher	1.2%	(4)
Denominational leader/ consultant	3.8%	(13)
None	2.6%	(9)

2. What is your ministry job title? (If a student, what is your planned job title?)

Only the top six titles are listed in descending order:

- senior pastor/minister (47 respondents)
- pastor (40)
- executive pastor (13)
- associate pastor (12)
- nonprofit executive director (8)
- president/CEO (7)

Many other titles were mentioned, but they were uniquely worded and didn't fit neatly into the above primary categories.

3. In what industry did you work before deciding to enter into ministry?

Accounting/finance	5.2%	(18)
Administrative/clerical	2.6%	(9)
Advertising/marketing/PR	2.3%	(8)
Aerospace/aviation/defense	1.2%	(4)
Agriculture, forestry, and fishing	1.5%	(5)
Arts, entertainment, and media	1.5%	(5)
Automotive/motor vehicle/parts	2.9%	(10)
Banking/mortgage	4.1%	(14)
Biotech and pharmaceutical	0.3%	(1)
Construction/facilities	5.5%	(19)
Consulting	2.3%	(8)
Consumer products	0.6%	(2)
Customer service	1.2%	(4)
Education/training	4.7%	(16)
Employment placement	0.6%	(2)
Engineering/architecture	3.2%	(11)
Executive/management	6.1%	(21)
Government	1.2%	(4)
Health care	5.8%	(20)
Hospitality/tourism/travel	2.6%	(9)
Human resources/recruiting	2.0%	(7)
Information technology and Internet	5.2%	(18)
Insurance	4.7%	(16)
Law enforcement/security	0.9%	(3)
Legal	1.5%	(5)
Manufacturing/operations	4.9%	(17)

Military	0.3%	(1)
Nonprofit	1.5%	(5)
Oil/gas/utilities	2.6%	(9)
Publishing/printing	1.7%	(6)
Purchasing/procurement	0.3%	(1)
Real estate	1.5%	(5)
Restaurant/food service	0.9%	(3)
Retail/wholesale	6.1%	(21)
Sales—corporate	4.9%	(17)
Science	0.6%	(2)
Sports and recreation	0.6%	(2)
Supply chain/logistics/transportation	2.0%	(7)
Telecommunications	2.6%	(9)

4. Do you still have a full- or part-time secular job?

Yes	26.7%	(92)
No	73.3%	(252)

5. What was your secular income level when you decided to enter the ministry?

Unemployed	0.6%	(2)
$0–15,000	4.7%	(16)
$15,001–30,000	13.7%	(47)
$30,001–45,000	21.5%	(74)
$45,001–60,000	19.8%	(68)
$60,001–100,000	22.1%	(76)
$100,001+	17.7%	(61)

6. What is your income level now?

Unemployed	4.4%	(15)
$0–15,000	11.3%	(39)
$15,001–30,000	18.3%	(63)
$30,001–45,000	26.5%	(91)
$45,001–60,000	23.0%	(79)
$60,001–100,000	14.8%	(51)
$100,001+	1.7%	(6)

7. In which decade did you decide to enter ministry?

1930s		(0)
1940s		(0)
1950s		(0)
1960s	0.9%	(3)
1970s	4.1%	(14)
1980s	12.8%	(44)
1990s	37.8%	(130)
2000+	44.5%	(153)

8. When you made that decision, how long had you been a Christian?

6 months (or fewer)	0.3%	(1)
7–12 months	0.6%	(2)
1–3 years	3.8%	(13)
4–7 years	6.1%	(21)
8–15 years	21.2%	(73)
16–25 years	27.3%	(94)
More than 25 years	40.7%	(140)

9. How long had you been in your industry before you switched to ministry?

6 months (or fewer)	3.8%	(13)
7–12 months	0.6%	(2)
1–3 years	7.3%	(25)
4–7 years	12.8%	(44)
8–15 years	35.2%	(121)
16–25 years	28.5%	(98)
More than 25 years	11.9%	(41)

10. How old were you when you decided to switch?

15–24	5.5%	(19)
25–34	27.9%	(96)
35–44	35.5%	(122)
45–54	23.8%	(82)
55–64	6.7%	(23)
65+	0.6%	(2)

11. What was your marital status at the time?

Married	81.1%	(279)
Single	13.1%	(45)
Widowed	0.3%	(1)
Separated/ divorced	5.5%	(19)

12. How many children did you have at the time?

0	20.3%	(70)
1	11.3%	(39)
2	30.5%	(105)
3	21.8%	(75)
4–6	14.8%	(51)
6+	1.2%	(4)

13. What was the age of your youngest child at the time?

Did not have any children	20.9%	(72)
Less than one year	5.8%	(20)
1–3 years	15.1%	(52)
4–10 years	23.5%	(81)
10–15 years	7.6%	(26)
15+	27.0%	(93)

14. Who did God use to influence your decision the most?

Spouse	13.7%	(47)
Immediate family member	2.9%	(10)
Other relative	1.2%	(4)
Friend	5.8%	(20)
Professor/school teacher	0.9%	(3)
Senior pastor/minister	28.8%	(99)
Sunday school teacher	0.6%	(2)
Other church leader	8.4%	(29)
Coworker	2.3%	(8)
No one in particular	28.8%	(99)
Other	6.7%	(23)

15. When did you begin pursuing further education or any type of ministry training?

Never	21.5%	(74)
Less than one year later	40.1%	(138)
Within 1–3 years	25.6%	(88)
Within 4–7 years	7.0%	(24)
Within 8–15 years	4.9%	(17)
More than 15 years later	0.9%	(3)

16. How long did you deliberate before you knew your decision was final?

A matter of hours	9.0%	(31)
1–7 days	7.6%	(26)
2–4 weeks	11.3%	(39)
2–12 months	41.0%	(141)
2–5 years	22.4%	(77)
6–10 years	5.8%	(20)
11–20 years	1.7%	(6)
21+ years	1.2%	(4)

17. How did your closest family members (including spouse) respond in general to your decision?

Very positively	52.6%	(181)
Somewhat positively	29.7%	(102)
Neutral	6.1%	(21)
Somewhat negatively	8.4%	(29)
Very negatively	3.2%	(11)

18. What is your gender?

Male	79.7%	(274)
Female	20.3%	(70)

19. What is your denomination?

Adventist	1.2%	(4)
Brethren	0.9%	(3)
Catholic	0.6%	(2)
Christian	20.9%	(72)
Church of Christ	2.6%	(9)
Episcopal	1.7%	(6)
Holiness	1.7%	(6)
Independent Fundamentalist	6.7%	(23)
Lutheran	3.2%	(11)
Mennonite	0.9%	(3)
Methodist	4.9%	(17)
Nazarene	1.5%	(5)
Other Baptists	11.9%	(41)
Pentecostal	13.7%	(47)
Presbyterian	4.9%	(17)
Southern Baptist	19.5%	(67)
Wesleyan	3.2%	(11)

20. What is your current marital status?

Married	88.7%	(305)
Single	7.0%	(24)
Widowed	0.6%	(2)
Separated/divorced	3.8%	(13)

21. In what region do you currently reside?

United Kingdom	0.6%	(2)
Europe	0.3%	(1)
United States	91.3%	(314)
Africa	2.0%	(7)
Australia/ Pacific Rim	1.5%	(5)
Latin America/ Caribbean		(0)
Canada	3.2%	(11)
Middle East/ Asia	1.2%	(4)

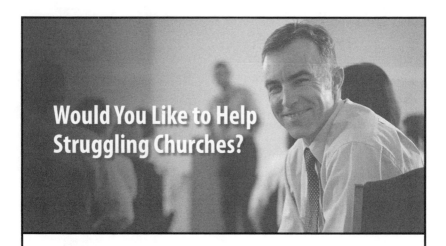

||||||||||||||

An Invitation

I pray you found this book useful—feel free to give me your feedback at tom@churchcentral.com. I may not be able to respond, but I do read all my e-mail, and your comments are welcome.

While you're at it, consider e-mailing me your answers to any or all of these questions:

1. Do you have a career crossover story of your own? If you've survived a wild adventure into ministry, send me a synopsis.

2. Would you like to receive a free guide to Church Central's consultant training program?

3. Are you a Christian business leader who has applied biblical business principles and experienced dramatic turnaround in your company? You can be part of our ongoing research in this area.

If any of these questions interests you, please drop me a line at tom@churchcentral.com. I'd love to hear from you.

Blessings on your business, ministry, family and future. God's hand is in every one of those areas, guiding your steps and granting wisdom to those who ask.

Now if any of you lacks wisdom, he should ask God,
who gives to all generously and without criticizing,
and it will be given to him.
JAMES 1:5